The Retention and Expansion
of Existing Businesses

The Retention
and Expansion
of
Existing Businesses

THEORY AND PRACTICE
IN BUSINESS VISITATION PROGRAMS

Edited by **GEORGE W. MORSE**

Contributors   JAMES P. MILLER
DANIEL OTTO
ELLEN HAGEY
JOHN D. ROHRER
WILLIAM GILLIS
ROBERT MCLAUGHLIN
MARION BENTLEY

IOWA STATE UNIVERSITY PRESS / AMES

©1990 Iowa State University Press, Ames, Iowa 50010

Manufactured in the United States of America

⊛ This book is printed on acid-free paper.

First edition, 1990

International Standard Book Number: 0-8138-0133-8

Library of Congress Cataloging-in-Publication Data

The retention and expansion of existing businesses : theory and practice in business visitation programs / edited by George W. Morse. - 1st ed.
    p.   cm.
    Includes index.
    ISBN 0-8138-0133-8
    1. Industrial promotion–United States. I. Morse, George Wilson, 1943–
HC110.I53R48 1990
338.973–dc20   89-11070

Contents

Contributors

GEORGE W. MORSE is Professor of Community Economics in the Department of Agricultural and Applied Economics at the University of Minnesota. When this book was written he was a community resource economist with the Ohio Cooperative Extension Service and an associate professor in the Department of Agricultural Economics and Rural Sociology at Ohio State University. From 1986 to 1989 Professor Morse directed the Ohio Business Retention and Expansion Program, cosponsored by the Ohio Department of Development and OSU's Cooperative Extension Service. Forty-one Ohio counties and nine other states have used the retention and expansion (R&E) program that he developed. He received his M.S. from Purdue University and his Ph.D. from the University of Wisconsin.

JAMES P. MILLER is an economist in the Economic Research Service, Washington, D.C. He has researched and written on a range of issues relating to small businesses and entrepreneurship in rural areas.

DANIEL OTTO is an Extension Service economist and associate professor in the Department of Economics, Iowa State University, Ames, Iowa. His R&E programs have focused on community economic analysis and planning and regional input/output analysis. He helped introduce the R&E program to Iowa.

ELLEN HAGEY is a research analyst with the Neighborhood Reinvestment Corporation in Washington, D.C. When this book was written she was a program consultant with the Ohio Business Retention and Expansion Program at Ohio State University. In that role, she trained community leaders for the program and coauthored the final R&E reports.

JOHN D. ROHRER is acting assistant director for community and natural resource development in the Ohio Cooperative Extension Service, Ohio State University. He has fifteen years' experience in community economic development extension programs.

WILLIAM GILLIS is an Extension Service economist and an associate professor in the Department of Agricultural Economics and Rural Sociology at Pennsylvania State University. He is currently director of the Center for Rural Pennsylvania, and he initiated the Pennsylvania R&E program.

ROBERT MCLAUGHLIN is professor of business, leadership, and community development at Goddard College in Plainfield, Vermont. He currently serves as chairperson of Goddard's Presidential Task Force on the Twenty-four Hour Curriculum. At the time of writing, he was doing doctoral research in the Department of Educational Policy and Leadership at Ohio State University.

MARION BENTLEY is an Extension Service economist and professor in the Department of Economics at Utah State University. He specializes in research and educational programs on plant closures, and he has also done research on small business incubators. He currently administers the Utah R&E visitation program in collaboration with the Utah Department of Commerce.

List of Tables

Preface

The popularity of business retention and expansion (R&E) as a local development strategy has skyrocketed since the early 1980s. With any new popular program there is a danger that it will be enthusiastically adopted without adequate background on the necessary prerequisites for success, leading to a large number of failures. This book, written for state development officials, local practitioners of local economic development, and community economics academicians describes the theoretical foundations, educational programs, and practical applications of the business R&E program–with the hope that informed enthusiasm will lead to successful local programs.

The goal of R&E programs is to stimulate local economic development by helping existing businesses increase their sales and employment, through a combination of programs that not only increase these firms' competitiveness but also improve the community's quality of life. The current R&E programs differ significantly from those adopted by communities during the 1960s and 1970s. The earlier programs were informal, unstructured, and marginally successful. They attempted only to improve the public relations between local firms and the community. Current R&E programs blend applied research with public relations and focus on both immediate action for resolving individual firm problems and long-term planning for improving the communities' overall business climate and the competitiveness of local firms. Although current R&E programs are more sophisticated and structured, they maintain considerable flexibility; consequently, their success and popularity have increased. At present, at least fifteen states have adopted and implemented technical assistance programs to assist communities starting these more highly structured local business visitation programs.

Many communities have R&E programs, but only 150 have the more structured, multiple-goal program described in this book. In your state,

how many communities have an R&E program that has: (1) surveyed at
least 30 firms using two visitors per visit? (2) handled the immediate
concerns of local firms with assistance from "Certified R&E Consultants"?
(3) had a task force that includes the mayor, a county commissioner, the
chamber of commerce director, a county extension agent, a banker, the
superintendent of a joint vocational school, and two other key leaders?
(4) produces a sixty- to ninety-page report that includes research on
employment trends, shift-share analysis, economic outlook information,
and summarizes the survey findings? and (5) develops a strategic planning
process? The communities on which this book is based can answer
positively to all these questions.

The authors bring the perspectives of both theory and practice to
their chapters. These chapters reflect their thirty-five years of experience
in helping more than two hundred communities with a wide range of
economic development strategies. The experiences described reflect the
perspectives of economic development professionals from utility companies, state government, and educational institutions. Geographically,
the examples come from Georgia, Idaho, Illinois, Iowa, Massachusetts,
New Jersey, Ohio, Pennsylvania, Utah, and Wisconsin.

In October 1985 Ohio State University sponsored a conference on
R&E titled "Community Economic Development Through the Retention
and Expansion of Existing Businesses." As a result of that conference, the
Ohio Cooperative Extension Service developed a hybrid model incorporating the best of the New Jersey and Ohio programs. This model was
field tested in 1986. With the exception of Chapters 2 and 12, this book
reflects the 1986–1989 field experiences with this hybrid model.

This book provides the first in-depth analysis of these new highly
structured R&E visitation teams. The theoretical base for the program
provides not only prescriptive guideposts but criteria for measuring
success or failure in the programs. The case studies provide initial
evidence that the program is rather robust under a variety of situations.
As one local leader put it, "The R&E program is a 'can't lose' program.
At the very least, we will show our firms that we appreciate them and
want to help them." The case studies suggest that the beneficial impacts
appear to go far beyond this public relations objective, which frankly is
usually the primary reason most communities initiate the program.

Part I, The Theoretical Foundations of R&E Visitation Programs,
presents a conceptual model for the R&E visitation program and
describes the impact of existing firms on regional growth. In Chapter 1,
George Morse defines R&E and provides a conceptual model for the
business visitation phase of an R&E program. This chapter argues that
R&E is more than a public relations program, more than an attempt to
help firms move out of the past, and more than simply improving firm
efficiency. In Chapter 2, James Miller provides empirical evidence to
contrast the impact on a community's economy from existing firms with
the impact from new firm start-ups. His findings support earlier research

that existing firms have a greater influence on local economic development than new firm start-ups.

Part II, Educational Programs, explains the objectives and methods of the educational/technical assistance programs provided to communities starting new R&E visitation programs. In Chapter 3, Daniel Otto, George Morse, and Ellen Hagey outline the status of current R&E programs and conclude that most states now recognize the importance of working with their existing businesses to stimulate economic development but that few have developed training programs for communities. In the latter part of this chapter, the training efforts of Georgia, New Jersey, and Ohio are outlined.

Morse and Hagey, in Chapter 4, present a chronological description of the steps involved in conducting a local R&E visitation program, based on their experience of working with more than forty-one communities. Morse, in Chapter 5, stresses the importance of supplementing the primary data gathered from the visitation program with secondary data. These secondary data cannot only give a more complete profile of the community's economy but can also help the local leaders to better understand the impact of global and national economic changes. John Rohrer and George Morse, in Chapter 6, explain the educational benefits of presenting the Economic Development Teleconference Series to communities. This series is a particularly important tool in small or remote areas. Finally, in Chapter 7 George Morse, William Gillis, and Daniel Otto explain the importance of the final report and the potential applications of the information gathered from the business visitation survey.

Part III, Successful Local R&E Visitation Programs, outlines the structure of successful local programs from five states. In Chapter 8 George Morse, Robert McLaughlin, and Ellen Hagey review the five objectives of the program and present examples from five states of the impacts of their R&E visitation programs. In Chapter 9, Morse describes the implementation process and the impacts of the R&E program in Washington County, Ohio–a rural area of 65,000 people.

In Chapter 10, Ellen Hagey then describes the successes of Champaign County, a small rural county in west central Ohio. As has been the case in many of the counties, one of the outcomes of the program was the establishment of an economic development position in the county. Robert McLaughlin, an educational policy analyst, describes his Ph.D. dissertation research on the social dynamics in one county that completed the R&E visitation program. As suggested by the title of Chapter 11, McLaughlin found that the local task force developed strong social, political, and epistomological connections as a result of the process that strengthened their ability to deal with economic development issues.

The final chapter by Marion Bentley recognizes that R&E visitation programs cannot retain all plants. In fact, since structural changes will force some plants to close, one of the objectives of the visits and the study of secondary data is to provide an early warning of plant closures. Bentley's chapter suggests means of assisting employees and communities when the initial goals of R&E are not achieved.

Guarding one's trade secrets in the art of attracting new firms to a state or locality is a well-known practice. However, in R&E the emphasis on helping existing firms engenders a new spirit of cooperation–not only between communities but also between states. Efforts to assist existing firms to become more efficient and competitive frequently requires cooperation and seldom results in neighbors "stealing" the firm. In fact, sharing one's experience in R&E can yield positive benefits as those assisted return with their own contributions. It is with this spirit of mutual cooperation that the authors share their experiences in helping small- to medium-size communities grow through the retention and expansion of their existing firms.

Acknowledgments

Over eight thousand people collaborated in the development of the local business retention and expansion (R&E) visitation program. Without local volunteer visitors, R&E consultants and coordinators, economic development professionals, and Cooperative Extension Service agents and specialists, this program would not have been possible.

The Ohio Department of Development and the Ohio Cooperative Extension Service have supported the Ohio Business Retention and Expansion Program financially since 1986. Both agencies have also contributed suggestions for improving the R&E concept.

The Ohio programs serve as the primary source of information used in this book. But ideas and examples also came from many other states. New Jersey, which independently developed a very similar program to the Ohio R&E program, helped the states of Wisconsin, Michigan, Georgia, and Pennsylvania develop their programs. Pennsylvania, Indiana, Iowa, Kansas, North Dakota, Oklahoma, and Arizona used the Ohio model. In every case ideas flowed both ways. The participating states contributed new approaches and educational tools.

A number of individuals contributed to the Ohio program and to the formation of the thoughts that went into this book. In the Ohio Cooperative Extension Service, Sam Crawford deserves special mention. Sam introduced me to R&E in 1981 and helped by discussing many of the ideas that went into our 1984 pilot programs. At the Ohio Department of Development, Howard Wise was the champion of the R&E idea from the earliest days. My research associate, Ellen Hagey, provided extremely valuable assistance during the first two critical years of program development. Dale Hileman, Columbia Gas of Ohio, and Michael Jay, Ohio Technology Transfer Organization, worked with several communities as R&E consultants and contributed significantly to the R&E program follow-up efforts. Donn Ellerbrock and Paul Clappsaddle lent the advice and counsel on both the local program and the funding process from the beginning.

The coordinators, consultants, and county agents in the earliest local programs had a major influence on the Ohio program. These included Diane Rutschilling and Joe Beiler from Mercer County; William Graham and Eric Norland from Medina County; Charles Manges from Wooster; and Bill Robison and Nancy Morcher from London, Ohio.

Since 1986 over two thousand local leaders have contributed to the Ohio Business Retention and Expansion Program. The coordinators, consultants, and Ohio Cooperative Extension agents working on this program from 1986 to late 1988 also had a major influence on the Ohio program. The coordinators included Earl Steinecker, Mike Hogan, Bruce Miller, Roland Patzer, Mary Lee Gecowets, Steven Prochaska, Dennis Baker, Terry Richardson, Michael Schultz, Bill Grunkemeyer, Phillip Houston, Renee Magee, Marianne Mrohaly, Eric Middlebrook, Carol Cilbersten, Amy Hookway, Terry Sterling, Don Foley, John Dete, Larry Brown, Mike Lloyd, Edward Geiger, Mort Ake, Walter Wehenkel, John Ulmer, Paul Doerr, Martin Kulhman, Oscar Decker, Emerson Shimp, and Christine Dietsch.

The consultants for these programs were Kurt Kuffner, Dale Hileman, Paul Clappsaddle, Laura Grove, Thomas Suter, Michael Jay, Sam Crawford, Bob Zetty, Earl Joy, Pat Landi, Dan Evers, James Boerke, Doug Graver, Ben Kenney, Len Smith, Larry Morehead, Lee Dorsey, Kenneth Lengieza, John Watkins, Jay Jacquet, Ray Schindler, Mary Ann Shatto, David Amstutz, Bob Fawcett, and Joy Wright. The Ohio Cooperative Extension Service agents providing leadership for these programs were John Smith, Mike Hogan, Jack Sommers, Steven Prochaska, Dennis Baker, Bill Grunkemeyer, Rick Grove, Gerald Mahan, Merlin Wentworth, Steve Bartels, Ken Lafontaine, Barbara Wurzel, Ken Simeral, Herbert Lane, Harold Schneider, Joyce Fittro, Mike Lloyd, Daryl Clark, Ray Wells, Neal Leimbach, John Ulmer, Tom Hopkins, Donald Kimmet, John Hixson, and Emerson Shimp.

The North Central Regional Center for Rural Development, located at Iowa State University, provided funding for the 1985 conference where this book originally started and some funding for Robert McLaughlin's 1987 research project on the effectiveness of the local programs. The Farm Foundation assisted in funding the 1985 conference as did the USDA Extension Service. The Aspen Institute for Humanistic Studies' Rural Economic Policy Program provided partial funding for the McLaughlin research. The Ohio Cooperative Extension Service and the Ohio Agricultural Research and Development Center provided the major support for the author in the development of this book.

A number of colleagues encouraged and challenged me to improve the original manuscript. Those who gave special assistance in improving the manuscripts are: Leroy Hushak, Fred Hitzhusen, Robert Backoff, Steven Gordon, William Gillis, and Dennis Henderson.

The acknowledgment would not be complete without thanking two excellent secretaries, Judy Petticord and Charlotte Walker, for their patience. And last but not least, I thank my wife, Elizabeth, for both her patience and encouragement when I worked evenings and weekends.

I

Theoretical Foundations
of R&E Programs

1

A Conceptual Model of Retention and Expansion Business Visitation Programs

GEORGE MORSE

Although "retention and expansion" (R&E) became a popular concept during the early 1980s and was considered the primary economic development concern by the Council of State Governments in 1981, it remains a poorly defined concept.[1] Lacking an explicit definition and conceptual model, the concept of R&E is difficult to critique, to measure, and to improve. This chapter attempts to define retention and expansion, presents a conceptual model for the business visitation phase of an R&E program, and describes the relationship between R&E and other economic development strategies.

DEFINITION OF RETENTION AND EXPANSION

The term *retention and expansion* has been used in a variety of narrow contexts. Two major definitions of R&E will be discussed here. First, R&E efforts, which often focus initially on the manufacturing sector rather than on the service sector, are interpreted as economic development strategies intended to regenerate the types of economic systems that existed twenty or thirty years ago. While many initial R&E programs do concentrate on assisting the declining manufacturing sector in a com-

3

munity rather than the growing service sector, their objective is not to recreate the economies of the 1950s. Rather, such programs are trying not only to assist a vital element in the local economy but also to help community leaders understand the structural changes that have occurred and continue to occur in their region. Manufacturing is still the leading employer in many communities despite significant restructuring in the past several years. Moreover, most manufacturers are export oriented; that is, they attract outside money to the community, which stimulates the local economy. Also, manufacturers tend to offer higher wages and employ more highly skilled employees than service businesses do. R&E programs also try to help communities better understand the structural changes within manufacturing because a well-informed community is better able to stimulate growth. Although manufacturing is declining, it is not disappearing; communities strongly tied to manufacturing need to adapt positively to its changing structure.

Second, R&E efforts, which often emphasize the importance of competitiveness to economic vitality, are viewed simply as economic development strategies intended to increase firm efficiency.[2] Increasing efficiency is only one of the program's potential results. It is, in fact, one potential result that is rarely stated explicitly. Promoting R&E solely as a means to increase efficiency is often poorly received by communities. They resent an "outsider" who presumes that their local businesses are inefficiently managed. Communities become much more receptive to the program if R&E is promoted as a means to increase their firms' "competitiveness" by reducing costs.

Although these two definitions are partially correct, they fail to convey the numerous objectives of an R&E program and the variety of ways such a program can be effective in stimulating economic development. *R&E programs are all local development efforts designed to assist and encourage existing local businesses to grow.* These efforts include:

1. increasing firm efficiency;
2. improving public relations between local government and local businesses;
3. improving the community's quality of life;
4. offering subsidies for the retention and expansion of firms;
5. influencing the retention and expansion of state and federal facilities;
6. creating an early-warning system for plant contractions, closings, and relocations; and
7. designing an overall long-term economic development strategy.

Increasing Firm Efficiency

Local leaders implementing an R&E program cannot directly increase a firm's efficiency (competitiveness); they can only encourage a firm to become more efficient. They do so by first identifying the firm's obstacles to greater efficiency and then by suggesting appropriate state programs or agencies or by establishi ng seminars that might help to remove those obstacles.

Improving Public Relations

Public relations is one of the most obvious and important means by which an R&E program can help stimulate business growth. Businesses want to be appreciated and respected by the community. If a community supports its businesses, that alone can be a significant noneconomic reason for a business not to relocate or close. A community, via an R&E program, helps to establish a healthy business climate by expressing its appreciation for the economic contributions made by its businesses and by maintaining open communication between businesses and local government.

Improving the Community's Quality of Life

There is considerable evidence that many businesses locate and remain in communities for noneconomic factors.[3] These reasons include the quality of education, recreational opportunities, housing availability, and other quality-of-life measures. An R&E program can help improve the quality of life in communities by identifying those features that are most attractive and those that need to be improved.

Offering Subsidies

Subsidies offered to retain or expand firms are not appealing to many local leaders and taxpayers. In some instances, however, subsidies may be a valuable development tool. From the local government and taxpayer perspective, a subsidy would be rational as long as the revenue forgone was less than the revenue gained owing to the subsidy.[4] Economists, and others who disregard subsidies as an R&E tool, abdicate their responsibility to indicate the relative efficiency and distributional impacts of alternative subsidies.[5]

Retaining and Expanding State and Federal Facilities

The retention and expansion of the defense industry, military bases, state prisons, and other state and federal installations is frequently a high priority in R&E programs. It is speculated that the retention and expansion of these facilities is based more on political than on economic reasons. Nonetheless, this goal should be recognized as a component of an R&E strategy.

Developing an Early Warning System

Developing an early warning system of plant closings, contractions, or relocations is vital to a community because it provides an opportunity for the community to prevent, or at least reduce, the negative impact of such actions. Since time is frequently the most limiting factor in efforts to save a plant or to adjust to a closing, developing an early warning system is a valuable component of an R&E program. Closings, contractions, and relocations are most likely to occur in very specialized manufacturing sectors when technology, new products, and new competitors increase competition.[6]

Designing Long-Term Strategy

While some of the previously mentioned examples, such as providing firms with information, can be performed on an individual basis, others may require communitywide programs or policies. Even the development of marketing and management seminars or consulting services for individual firms may require community support. Major decisions on the directions economic development efforts should take can be facilitated by a carefully implemented strategic planning effort. The R&E program provides a means of developing a strategic plan for economic development.[7]

THE CONCEPTUAL MODEL OF THE R&E BUSINESS VISITATION PROGRAM

R&E programs do much more than simply recreate old structures of economies or increase firm efficiency. Business R&E covers a wide range of educational programs and assistance to existing firms, including business management, marketing strategies, labor training, labor/management relations, and financial programs. There are so many R&E options available to communities that priorities must be set for those that will receive major attention at given points. The R&E Visitation Program is an excellent means of setting these priorities.

An R&E visitation program is an action-oriented, strategic planning process for identifying the concerns of existing local firms, for understanding the economic outlook of the community, for setting priorities among competing local economic development programs, and for developing the potential support needed to implement these goals.

The ultimate goals of the R&E business visitation program are:

1. expanding local firms;
2. retaining local firms;

3. providing rapid assistance to communities (employees, businesses) adjusting to plant closures, contractions, or relocations; and
4. attracting new firms.

Of the four, of course, retention and expansion have the greatest priority. If these goals are not met, however, the third goal gains first priority. The fourth goal may seem somewhat out of place since R&E programs focus on existing businesses. Nonetheless, the data collected and the probusiness attitude demonstrated during the program can help a community market itself to attract new industry. The rest of this section describes the relationship between these ultimate goals and the R&E visits, describing the ways communities can use the data collected on the visits to achieve these goals.

Expansion and Retention of Existing Businesses

Figure 1.1 presents a conceptual model of the R&E business visitation program. Beginning at the right side of the figure, the expansion and retention of existing businesses is a function of not only economic but also noneconomic factors. Specifically, public relations, quality of life, and profit levels influence the expansion and retention of businesses.

CONCEPTUAL MODEL OF THE R&E BUSINESS VISITATION PROGRAM

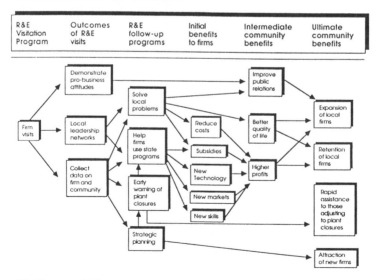

Figure 1.1. Conceptual Model of the R&E Business Visitation Program.

Improving Public Relations and Quality of Life

Improving public relations, improving the quality of life, and increasing profits are all intermediate goals of the R&E visitation program. Realization of these goals depends on the preceding accomplishments of the program (columns 1 through 4). In other words, to improve public relations, local leaders must either help solve local government problems for the businesses (column 3) or demonstrate the community's probusiness attitude by simply conducting the visit (columns 1 and 2). The former cause-effect relationship has a stronger impact on public relations than the latter. Improving the quality of life (column 5) is also a function of the local leaders' ability to solve local government problems (column 3).

Increasing Profits

Increasing profits (column 5) is a function of several initial benefits the firms receive from an R&E visitation program. Higher profits stem from reduced costs per unit (and/or increased revenues) and can be influenced by R&E visitation program efforts (column 3). If, for example, the R&E visitation program is able to solve government problems or introduce state or federal development programs to local businesses and the businesses are able to capitalize on this assistance by reducing costs, receiving subsidies, adopting new technology, entering new markets, or learning new skills, they could increase profits. With greater profits, the businesses are more likely to remain or expand in their current location.

Regardless of the economic structure of the industry, two supply-side factors can lead to increased profits for early adopters.[8] Technology and lower factor prices (column 4) can reduce the average unit costs for firms. These reduced costs may allow the firm to become more price-competitive and better able to capture a larger share of the national or international market. Conversely, firms that do not reduce unit costs may lose market share, and thus be forced to reduce employment.

Although new technology frequently involves the partial substitution of capital for labor, it is clear that firms cannot remain competitive if they do not adopt appropriate technology. Retaining an existing, competitive firm by helping it adopt new technology may cause the loss of some jobs, but this scenario is better than the loss of the plant and all of its jobs.

This logic implies that a local R&E effort should help firms use state and federal programs that reduce costs through: (1) the acquisition of technical knowledge, (2) labor training, (3) management orientation, and (4) labor-management improvements. Communities that assist firms in such a way increase their locational attractiveness.

Shifts in the demand-side are equally important in determining a firm's profitability. Demand shifters include: (1) the prices of complementary goods and services, (2) the prices of substitute goods, (3) the average household income, (4) the distribution of income, (5) the size of the population, (6) the composition or age structure of the population, (7) the labor force participation rates, and (8) tastes and preferences. Shifts in any of these factors can lead to opportunities to increase or pressures to decrease output.

Especially for smaller firms, staying informed about all of these changes and adjusting to all of these factors can be difficult. While there is little that communities can do to influence the demand shifters, they can develop newsletters, organize seminars, and hold workshops that help firms understand these changes. Seminars on demographics and market shifts ease the cost burden on firms that would otherwise have tried to obtain this information themselves. Although few communities can create the above programs by themselves, they can gain some of the programs' benefits by working with state and federal agencies and state universities.

Solving Problems and Introducing Programs

To help solve government problems and to introduce development programs to its businesses (column 3), the R&E task force must demonstrate its probusiness attitude to establish trust and credibility, develop an extensive network of economic development professionals, and collect information about the businesses and community (column 2). Demonstration of the probusiness attitude occurs when the visits are made and the local leadership networks are developed as the key players in the program become more united. The R&E visitation program includes a wide range of local leaders, often including several communities within a county. Both public and private sector leaders work together during the business visits. Through this cooperative effort, development of leadership skills may provide the greatest impacts on future growth. Using a survey during the business visits allows the community to collect data about the businesses.

Strategic Planning

In addition to tackling many problems immediately, the R&E visitation program does strategic planning on those concerns requiring more time and resources. A task force of key private and public sector leaders meets six or more times to evaluate the strengths and weaknesses of their community from the perspective of their existing local businesses. To put changes in their community into a national and international perspective, the task force reviews information from the *U.S. Industrial Outlook* and employment trends in their community relative to the state and nation. Specific recommendations for local action are developed by the task force after a discussion of the feasibility of different options. These are published in a final report (see Chapter 7) and shared with the community in the final public meeting (see Chapter 4).

Early Warning Systems for Plant Closings

Structural changes in the economy will force some firms to contract or even close. R&E programs that collect data about the economic outlook of local industries and factors influencing profits of individual establishments can provide an early warning of potential plant closures. Early warnings provide the opportunity to explore the options for using state programs to assist firms, to check the feasibility of new ownership or employee buy-outs, or to examine the possibility of using the plant for other uses. Even if the plant cannot be saved, early warnings allow the community more time to adjust to the plant closing.

Providing rapid assistance to those adjusting to plant closings, contractions, or relocations is a result of establishing an early warning system to such closings (see Figure 1.1). Theoretically the system is established during the follow-up stage of the visitation process. Although an early warning system may not always prevent plant closings, contractions, or relocations, it can reduce the devastation for those involved. The early warning system, in turn, depends upon the information gathered during the business visitation phase.

Demonstrating a Probusiness Attitude

The firm visits themselves are successful in demonstrating a probusiness attitude. With very few exceptions, firm representatives express pleasure and gratitude to the visitors for making the visit. This outcome of the R&E visitation program is universally recognized and articulated by local leaders at the start of the program. In most cases local leaders are uncertain about their abilities to achieve the other outcomes and follow-up programs. Consequently, this positive outcome helps motivate local leaders during the early stages of the program.

Local Leadership Networks

Neither the short-term assistance to firms nor the strategic plans can be implemented without a strong local leadership network. In many communities turf battles between groups make this network ineffective. As outlined in Chapter 4, several steps are taken to ensure that local groups work together on the R&E program. As pointed out in Chapter 8, the development of cooperation between local leaders and groups is frequently a key benefit of the R&E program. Through the involvement of key local leaders for the strategic planning process, political support is developed for the final recommendations (i.e., strategic plan).

Data Collection on Firm and Community

One of the primary purposes of the business visits is to collect data on the firms and their concerns. While the amount of data collected from each firm varies between states, it represents a major type of data in all cases. For example, in Ohio over 125 pieces of data are collected. Together with data from secondary sources (outlined in Chapter 5), the survey data form the information base for the strategic planning exercises.

Attraction of New Firms

Attracting new firms (column 6) depends on the strategic planning that is developed during the follow-up stage of an R&E program (column 3). The R&E visitation program assists communities in attracting new firms in four ways:

1. Local leaders in small- to medium-size communities become more familiar with the concerns of manufacturing businesses, leading to a better understanding of the advantages and disadvantages of their communities as locations for business
2. Local leaders develop the teamwork needed to conduct effective attraction programs
3. Communities remove some "turf" barriers that have reduced the effectiveness of industrial attraction efforts previously
4. Public relations between businesses and local government improves, which increases the chances of existing businesses telling prospective relocating businesses about the community's probusiness climate

In small- to medium-size communities there are few opportunities to host manufacturing prospects. This makes it difficult to maintain a well-informed and motivated hosting team. Participation in the R&E visitation team makes local leaders aware of some of the issues with which new firms may be concerned. Further, teamwork is essential in attracting new firms, but in small towns teamwork is frequently weak. The R&E visitation program requires and fosters teamwork.

Knowledge of the weaknesses in the community as a location for various types of manufacturing and other businesses can be useful in targeting attraction efforts. Further, the identification of the community's major and minor disadvantages as a location for business enables the community to try to improve its locational attractiveness.

Knowing the community's advantages as a location for business provides local leaders with essential marketing information. It also allows the community to target those firms or sectors for which it has a comparative advantage in terms of location.

Various local leaders find it easy to collaborate on R&E visitation programs, possibly because the stakes are not quite as high as when trying to attract a plant employing several hundred or even thousands of people. By eliminating "turf" problems through cooperation, the leaders can offer both existing and new firms the best range of services possible.

This reduction in turf conflicts is most apparent in countywide R&E programs. As local leaders have testified, these countywide efforts are often the first opportunities for chambers of commerce and city governments to conduct a joint economic development program. Before the birth of the R&E program it was next to impossible to even assemble leaders from separate communities to plan a unified attraction program. Now, several communities are exploring this possibility.

Once firms reach the final stage of industrial location decisions, they generally visit the communities in contention. One of the key components of this trip is the private visit between representatives of the new firm and representatives of existing businesses. Conveying a positive attitude toward the community as an excellent business location will help convince the new firm that the location is not only appropriate, but also desirable. One of the R&E visitation program's objectives is to give existing firms every reason for having a positive attitude toward their location.

In summary, this conceptual model suggests three immediate outcomes of the R&E visitation program (see Figure 1.1). These are:

1. demonstration of the community's probusiness attitude;
2. development of local leadership networks and skills in economic development; and
3. collection of data on existing firms and the community.

Also, the visitation program generates four follow-up programs intended to continue a community's R&E efforts (see Figure 1.1). These are:

1. assistance in solving local government problems;
2. assistance in using state and federal development programs;
3. establishment of early warning systems for plant closings, contractions, and relocations; and
4. preparation of a strategic plan for economic development.

The conceptual model of the business visitation phase represents only one part of an R&E program. Other parts strongly linked to this phase include programs about labor-management relations, marketing strategies, management seminars, export development workshops, and technology transfer programs. The R&E visitation program provides a means of setting priorities on these programs and building the community support needed for their implementation.

RELATIONSHIP OF R&E TO OTHER DEVELOPMENT STRATEGIES

Pulver has suggested the following five broad economic development strategies:[9]

1. Improve efficiency of existing firms
2. Improve a community's ability to capture dollars
3. Attract new basic employers
4. Encourage business formation
5. Increase aid received from broader governments

A complete community economic development program will include all five of these strategies. If the community cannot do them all at once, where should it start? And how does R&E fit into these strategies? Are there reasons to do R&E before or after other strategies?

R&E and Efficiency

Helping firms improve their efficiency or competitiveness by introducing them to state and federal programs is clearly one of the major goals of all R&E programs. As outlined earlier, educational programs on management, labor/management relations, financing, new technology, and labor training are all excellent candidates. The R&E visitation program helps to identify the specific types of other efforts that should be undertaken in the community.

Capturing Local Spending

This option refers to increasing the amount of local spending by consumers, other producers, and tourists. To a small degree the R&E visitation program captures data that are useful in this strategy. The R&E survey asks local firms if there are any raw materials, supplies, or intermediate products that they believe could be produced economically in the area. This data can be used to encourage the local production of new products or increase the number of services available, reducing the amount of spending leakage.

Other aspects of this strategy, however, are competitive with the R&E visitation program. Attempts to encourage local purchases take organizational time and effort. Local leaders must evaluate whether or not the payoffs are greater for changes in local shopping patterns or in working primarily with existing industries. Leaders at the state or national level also must determine the degree to which this strategy is primarily a "zero-sum game"; that is, the degree to which benefits in the form of additional local purchases for one community are realized at the expense of fewer expenditures in neighboring communities.

Attraction of New Basic Employers

There are clear connections between R&E, especially the R&E visitation program, and attraction efforts. First, the R&E visitation program helps local leaders understand the features of their community that are most attractive to new firms as well as those that need correction. Second, the data on the strengths of the community can be used in promotional pieces about the community. Third, the experience gained by the local leaders in an R&E visitation program proves valuable when hosting new firms. Fourth, satisfied local firms are a prerequisite to a successful hosting of new firms. The R&E visitation program can identify problems with existing firms and work toward their resolution, improving the odds that visits between new firms and existing ones will be positive experiences. Fifth, the data on firm products and input purchases can be used to suggest forms of local import substitution.

Should an R&E visitation program be done simultaneously with an attraction effort, before it, or after it? Communities never want to ignore prospective firms that are considering them as a potential site. However, mounting an attraction effort before an R&E effort does so without the benefits of the data collected from local firms.

Encourage Business Formation

This strategy focuses on helping entrepreneurs start new firms with new products or services. There is one philosophical difference and one practical difference between R&E and the encouragement of entrepreneurship. The philosophical difference is one of emphasis. The R&E program is likely to emphasize those activities that help firms become more efficient in their production and marketing. The business formation program is likely to emphasize the location of market niches and prerequisites to the formation of a new venture.

The practical difference is one of industry focus. In practice, although not necessarily in theory, the R&E program focuses on manufacturing firms. In practice, but again not in theory, business formation programs tend to focus on retail, wholesale, and service industries. While a "pure" business formation program might put greater emphasis on the "new" business than would an R&E visitation program, there is tremendous overlap. Once a business has an address and a phone number, it is likely to be included in the R&E program. Then the R&E program will attempt to assist the new business as much as the older ones.

Increase Aid Received from Broader Governments

Pulver describes this strategy as one in which a community attempts to get back some of the dollars taxed away by broader "governmental units, and if possible, to acquire dollars taxed by wealthier areas." This includes attracting *or retaining* state and national government employers. It might also include attracting *or retaining* retirement villages, medical facilities, or nursing homes. In other cases, it involves taking full advantage of state and federal aid for infrastructure development (e.g., streets, sewers, water systems, schools, and parks).

Most R&E visitation programs, especially in smaller counties, visit large governmental employers, large medical facilities, large nursing homes, and large retirement centers. Further, nearly every R&E program makes recommendations with respect to infrastructure.

Complements or Competitors

Should the community attempt to conduct all five strategies at once? Or more accurately, should a community attempt to initiate new efforts in all five at once? Or should they be phased in? If phased in, which should be done first?

As the reader proceeds through the book, he or she will develop an appreciation for the claim that only one of these five strategies should be developed at a time. Furthermore, since the R&E program lays the groundwork for a solid attraction program, the R&E effort should precede attraction efforts. By helping local leaders understand the needs of their major local firms, efforts to assist entrepreneurs are likely to be more successful after the R&E visitation program has been conducted. Priorities on attempts to increase state and federal aid can also flow out of the visits, suggesting that R&E visitation should precede expanded efforts here.

The question of whether or not a community ought to work extensively with retail and service sector firms in reducing leakages is related to two factors. First, the jobs per firm are usually much higher in manufacturing firms than in the retail and service sectors, giving the R&E program a greater potential impact. Second, there is the nagging question of whether or not the retail trade work is really just a "zero-sum game."[10]

SUMMARY

Business visitation programs will be more effective if the definition of R&E is explicit, if practitioners and educators understand the conceptual model, and if the linkages of the visitation program to other economic development efforts, such as early warning systems and attraction efforts, are understood.

R&E programs are defined as all those local development efforts that are aimed at facilitating and encouraging the growth of existing businesses.

The conceptual model illustrates graphically the linkages between the visits and the ultimate objectives of the program, which include the retention and expansion of firms; rapid assistance to those involved in adjusting to plant closings, contractions, and relocations; and the attraction of new firms.

While any complete local economic development program involves at least five broad strategies, R&E visitation programs are an excellent place to start such a program.

NOTES

1. Preliminary results presented at the conference "Rural Development Strategies in the '80s," sponsored by the National Association of State Development Agencies in Lexington, Kentucky, Dec. 1986.

2. Glen C. Pulver, "A Theoretical Framework for the Analysis of Community Economic Development Policy," in *Nonmetropolitan Industrial Growth and Community Change*, ed. Gene F. Summers and Arne Selvik (Lexington, Mass.: Lexington Books, 1979).

3. Robert Ady, Senior Vice President of the Fantus Company, the nation's major industrial location consulting firm, reports that Fantus recommends the least-cost location only half of the time owing to the importance of these noneconomic factors. Cheryl A. Farr, ed., *Shaping the Local Economy* (Washington, D.C.: International City Management Assoc., 1984), 83.

4. George W. Morse and Michael C. Farmer, "Location and Investment Effects of a Tax Abatement Program," *Nation Tax Journal* (June 1986).

5. Farr, *Shaping the Local Economy*, 1984.

6. See Chapter 12 for strategies for coping with failure in R&E.

7. The linkages between strategic planning and business R&E are described in more detail in George W. Morse, "Implementing Strategic Economic Planning in Small Communities Via Business R&E Programs: A Research Outline," (Columbus, Oh.: Dept. of Agricultural, Economic, and Rural Sociology, Ohio State University, Dec. 1986).

8. The reactions to changes in profits is the most rapid in competitive industries. In the long run, both oligopolistic and monopolistic firms must adopt cost-reducing technology to survive and expand.

9. Pulver, "A Theoretical Framework."

10. For an excellent discussion of the conditions under which local economic development is likely to be a zero sum game, see Ron Shaffer, *Community Economics* (Ames, Ia.: Iowa State Univ. Press, 1980).

REFERENCES

Ady, Robert M. "Shifting Factors in Plant Location." In *Shaping the Local Economy*, ed. Cheryl A. Farr. Washington, D.C.: International City Management Assoc., 1984.

Farr, Cheryl A., ed. *Shaping the Local Economy*, Washington, D.C.: International City Management Assoc., 1984.

Morse, George W. "Implementing Strategic Economic Planning in Small Communities via Business R&E Programs: A Research Outline." Columbus, Oh.: Ohio State University, Dept. of Agricultural Economic and Rural Sociology, Dec. 1986.

___, and Michael C. Farmer. "Location and Investment Effects of a Tax Abatement Program." *National Tax Journal.* June 1986, 229–36.

Pulver, Glen C. "A Theoretical Framework for the Analysis of Community Economic Development Policy." In *Nonmetropolitan Industrial Growth and Community Change*, ed. Gene F. Summers and Arne Selvik. Lexington, Mass.: Lexington Books, 1979.

Shaffer, Ron. *Community Economics.* Ames, Ia.: Iowa State Univ. Press, 1989.

2

Business Expansion and Retention in the Great Lakes States, 1976-1980

JAMES P. MILLER

The continued good economic health of businesses already located in a community is vital. Existing businesses that remain competitive provide the community with continuing employment, income, and tax revenue. They may also be the most cost-effective source of new employment. Business incentive programs to either attract new businesses from outside the community or encourage local entrepreneurship are often more expensive and have lower payoffs than business retention programs.

The purpose of this chapter is to investigate a series of questions regarding the importance of existing businesses in the job generation process in the East North Central (ENC) census division (Wisconsin, Illinois, Michigan, Indiana, and Ohio) from 1976 to 1980. The phrase **job generation process** refers to the relative contribution of business start-ups, closings, and expansions to total employment growth. The objective is to gain greater knowledge about how to respond to the recent loss of jobs in the Great Lakes states and how to generate more secure jobs in the future.

How important are existing businesses in creating new jobs? Do expansions by existing businesses contribute more to employment than the attraction of new businesses? As important as existing businesses are,

relatively little research has been done regarding their potential to create
jobs compared to business start-ups or migrants from other states. In
1979 David Birch of the Massachusetts Institute of Technology, who
pioneered the research methods used in this study, found in his national
study that existing firms created more jobs than new firms.[1] This finding
was confirmed in three subsequent studies. The first was by Miller in
1980, who found that all of the net employment growth in the manufacturing sector from 1969 to 1975 was due to existing plant operations. A
second study by the Wisconsin Department of Development concluded
that the "vast majority" of job gains in Wisconsin from 1969 to 1981 came
from existing businesses, and a third (by Armington) in 1986 reported
that 60 percent of the new jobs in independent firms and 52 percent of
the new jobs in branch plants were in expansions.[2]

What role does size, ownership status, and industrial sector play in job
generation and the survival of existing businesses? Are existing firms
more likely to survive as their employment size increases and, if they do
survive, are they more likely to expand or contract employment? Do
locally owned, independent businesses create more jobs than corporate
affiliates? Do they have a higher survival rate than corporate affiliates?
Does the location of a corporate headquarters in the North make a
difference? How do existing businesses perform in the service and trade
sectors compared to manufacturing? Are they the primary sources of new
jobs and what are their chances for survival?

The consensus from recent studies and articles on the subject of
business size and ownership and its impact on the regional, state, or local
economy generally favors small, local ownership. Previous studies by
Birch, Miller, and others show that the smaller the business, the more
jobs it will generate. Birch, for example, found that small business
establishments—those with fewer than one hundred employees—generated
about 82 percent of the net employment growth in the United States
from 1969 to 1976.[3] Locally owned businesses generated over 50 percent
of the net new jobs. Corporate affiliates created fewer jobs than local
businesses, and according to Birch, affiliates were a more "volatile source"
of employment, that is, affiliates had lower survival rates and higher rates
of job losses due to closings. This finding was supported by the results
of other studies. Smith, for example, found that externally owned
manufacturing plants had a much higher closure rate than locally owned
plants in the North from 1969 to 1973.[4]

Business ownership—the distinction between locally owned businesses
and those controlled by management outside the community or
region—has become an important issue, particularly in states and
communities that have lost jobs because of closings and layoffs by
national and multinational corporations. In a recent article, Reamer
observes that where there is a high proportion of absentee-owned
affiliates such as in South Carolina and Arkansas, "the economy is
vulnerable to disinvestment decisions which are made with little or no

concern about the local consequences."[5] Locally owned businesses, on the other hand, tend to stay put and keep more proprietary income and investment circulating in the community. In addition, because they have a vested interest in the community, locally owned businesses are more responsible to their workers. They often adjust to hard times by cutting wages and hours rather than by laying off workers as absentee-owned affiliates tend to do. In a related article on absentee-ownership in the Tennessee Valley region, Jane Jacobs believes that the problem of declining regions cannot be solved by "luring branch plants of multi-national corporations or other enterprises up for grabs."[6] Transplanted, absentee-owned branch plants generally do not reduce a declining region's dependence on imports. Her prescription is to promote small, local enterprises that will eventually replace imports.

How important are existing businesses in generating new jobs in nonmetropolitan counties? What types of existing businesses generate jobs in nonmetropolitan areas: small or large? locally owned or corporate affiliate? in manufacturing or in the service sector? How do business survival rates compare?

Previous studies of the job generation process and the ownership structure of businesses in rural areas focused primarily on manufacturing. Miller, in his national study, found that manufacturing plants in operation in 1969 provided the margin of difference between stable employment in nonmetropolitan counties and declining employment in metropolitan counties from 1969 to 1975.[7] Employment did not decline in non-metropolitan counties because job expansion by existing plants offset job losses from plant closings. On the other hand, employment did decline in metropolitan counties because expansion by existing plants was insufficient to offset job losses due to closings. In a subsequent study of rural plant closings in Iowa, Barkley and Anderson found that absentee-owned corporate affiliates were more likely to close and relocate than locally owned plants.[8] Local plants are "more susceptible to locational inertia" than absentee-owned plants. They are more likely to continue to operate under financial conditions that are unacceptable to absentee owners.

OVERVIEW OF THE ANALYSIS

This study examines the retention and growth performance of existing businesses—those businesses in operation in 1976 and still open in 1980—and closings in the East North Central (ENC) census division. The criteria selected to measure their performance over the 1976–1980 period are the survival rate and the employment expansion rate.

The tabulations in the section below were developed from a large database—U.S. Establishment and Enterprise Microdata (USEEM)—created by the Brookings Institution for the United States Small Business

Administration to investigate the growth behavior of small businesses. The USEEM files contain microdata (individual establishment records) on most private-sector businesses in the United States, about five million establishments, for the years 1976 and 1980. The files were derived from Dun and Bradstreet (Dun's Market Identifier) files.[9]

The tables show the relative contribution of different types of businesses (as defined by their employment size, ownership status and industrial sector) to the generation of jobs by either existing businesses expanding or new businesses starting up. The tables also show to what extent jobs were lost by existing businesses either cutting back employment or closing. Because their number is small, business relocations are not identified as separate categories. Business immigrants are included as start-ups and outmigrants are counted with closings. The major categories of business are:

Size (in 1976)
    Very small − 1 to 19 jobs
    Small − 20 to 99 jobs
    Medium − 100 to 999 jobs
    Large − 1000 or more jobs

Ownership (in 1976)
    Local − locally owned, independent, nonmulti-unit affiliated (single location)
    Regional affiliate − corporate branch or subsidiary with headquarters in the North Central census region: Ohio, Michigan, Indiana, Illinois, Wisconsin, Minnesota, Iowa, Missouri, North Dakota, South Dakota, Nebraska, and Kansas
    Nonregional affiliate − corporate branch or subsidiary with headquarters outside the North Central census region

Sector (based on one-digit standard industrial classification)
    Agriculture, forestry, fishing, and mining
    Construction
    Manufacturing
    Transportation, communications, and utilities
    Trade (wholesale and retail)
    Finance, insurance, and real estate
    Services

RESULTS

Small businesses—those establishments with less than one hundred employees—generated most of the jobs in the ENC census division (Table 2.1).

TABLE 2.1. Sources of Employment Change, East North Central (ENC) Census Division,* 1976–1980

Item	1976 employees millions	Net Change, 1976–80 employees millions	rate** percent
United States	76.2	11.2	15.3
ENC Division	15.5	1.4	9.2
Business Size			
Very small	3.4	.9	26.9
Small	3.6	.6	16.6
Medium	4.9	.2	4.8
Large	3.6	−.3	−8.8
Business Ownership			
Local	5.6	.5	9.0
Regional Affiliate	6.9	.7	10.6
Nonregional Affiliate	3.0	.2	6.7
Business Sector			
Manufacturing	5.5	.2	3.3
Trade and Services	7.1	1.0	14.0
Other	2.9	.2	8.9

*East North Central Division–Wisconsin, Illinois, Indiana, Michigan, and Ohio.
**The rate of net change was computed before rounding off to millions.

Size (based on employment size of establishment in 1976):
    Very small: 1 to 19 jobs
    Small: 20 to 99 jobs
    Medium: 100 to 999 jobs
    Large: 1000 or more jobs

Ownership (status of establishment in 1976):
    Local: Locally owned, independent, nonmulti-unit affiliate (single location)
    Regional affiliate: Corporate branches and subsidiaries with headquarters in the North Central census region
    Nonregional affiliate: Branches and subsidiaries with headquareters outside the North Central region

Sector (based on 1-digit Standard Industrial Classifications)

- Very small businesses—those with less than twenty employees—
  were the most active employers from 1976 to 1980. They
  generated the largest share of net new jobs and expanded
  employment at a faster rate than all other businesses combined.
- Employment in large businesses—those with one thousand or
  more employees—declined.

Most of the net employment growth was generated by either locally
owned businesses or corporate affiliates with headquarters in the North
Central census region (Table 2.1).

- Nonregional affiliates were not the major source of net
  employment growth.

Businesses in the trade and service sectors led the way in generating
additional jobs (Table 2.1).

- Manufacturing employment increased, but at a very low rate.

Existing businesses—those in operation in 1976 and still in business
in 1980—were very important in the job generation process.

- Existing businesses created about the same number of new jobs
  through expansions as new enterprises that started up or
  migrated from other states (Table 2.2).
- Employment cutbacks (contractions) by existing businesses
  eliminated fewer jobs than business closings.
- Existing businesses were the most important source of new jobs
  in almost every major industrial sector. From 1976 to 1980,
  business expansions created new jobs at a faster rate than start-
  ups in every sector except trade (Table 2.3). In addition,
  employment cutbacks by existing businesses eliminated fewer jobs
  than business closings in every sector except agriculture, forestry,
  and mining.

Business size played an important role in business expansion and
retention.

- The smaller the existing business, the more likely it is to
  generate jobs through expansion and the less likely it is to lose
  jobs through contraction (Table 2.3).
- On the other hand, the smaller the business, the less likely it is
  to survive. The rate of survival decreases and the rate of job loss
  progressively increases, the smaller the business.

TABLE 2.2. Components of Change in the Private Sector, East North Central Census Division, 1976–1980

Item	1976	Establishments (thousands)			
		Start-ups	Expansions	Closings	Contractions
United States	4,500.1	1,444.0	1,115.9	1,126.0	605.0
(Rate*)		(32.1)	(24.8)	(25.0)	(13.4)
ENC Division	803.3	227.9	198.4	195.5	114.8
(Rate*)		(28.2)	(24.5)	(24.1)	(14.2)
		Employment (millions)			
United States	76.2	16.6	16.9	13.6	8.9
(Rate**)		(21.7)	(22.2)	(17.9)	(10.7)
ENC Division	15.1	2.8	2.8	2.5	1.6
(Rate**)		(18.2)	(18.2)	(16.5)	(10.5)

*Percent of 1976 establishments.
**Percent of 1976 employment.

Business ownership is another important factor in retention.

- The more distant the corporate ownership of an affiliate, the less likely it is to survive. Locally owned businesses had the highest survival rate. The rate was lower for regional affiliates and lowest for affiliates with headquarters outside the North (Table 2.3).

Thus both size and ownership were important factors. The smaller the business and the more absentee the ownership, the less likely it is to survive.

- Very small, nonregional affiliates, as a group, had the lowest survival rate whereas large, locally owned businesses had the highest (Tables 2.4, 2.5, and 2.6).

TABLE 2.4. Rates of Job Gains Due to Business Expansions, East North Central (ENC) Census Division, 1979–1980

Business Size	Business Ownership Status (%)			
	Local	Regional Affiliate	Nonregional Affiliate	Total
Very Small	23.4	40.9	51.9	28.8
Small	16.0	26.8	31.2	22.9
Medium	11.6	16.6	11.8	14.2
Large	10.0	10.4	4.1	8.9
TOTAL	17.9	19.4	15.8	18.2

*Percent of 1976 employment.

TABLE 2.3. Sources and Components of Net Employment Change, East North Central Census Division, 1976–1980

Item	1976 Employees Millions	Employment Rate of Change* Due to:				Business Survival Rate**
		Start-ups	Expansions	Closings	Contractions	
United States	76.2	21.7	22.2	17.9	10.7	75.0
ENC Division	15.5	18.1	18.2	16.5	10.5	75.9
Business Size						
Very Small	3.4	26.6	28.8	21.8	6.8	74.9
Small	3.6	20.0	22.9	17.7	8.6	82.0
Medium	4.9	16.7	14.2	15.1	11.0	84.3
Large	3.6	10.0	8.9	12.2	15.5	87.9
Business Ownership						
Local	5.6	14.0	17.9	13.9	9.1	77.4
Regional Affiliate	6.9	19.3	19.4	15.9	12.2	73.0
Nonregional Affiliate	3.0	23.0	15.8	22.7	9.5	67.0
Business Sector						
Manufacturing	5.5	14.8	15.3	16.0	10.8	78.8
Trade***	3.6	25.6	15.0	20.8	9.4	71.6
Services	3.5	17.4	22.0	12.9	8.8	81.0
Construction	.7	17.0	22.1	18.3	13.1	75.6
Agriculture, Forestry, Mining	.2	18.9	28.8	11.7	14.4	84.6
TCU****	1.0	15.5	18.6	16.1	12.6	76.0
FIRE*****	1.0	14.8	26.3	16.3	14.3	81.0

*Percent of 1976 employment.

**Percent of 1976 establishments that did not close, 1876–1980.

****Trade: Wholesale and retail.

*****TCU: Transportation, Communications, and Utilities.

*****FIRE: Finance, Insurance, and Real Estate.

TABLE 2.5. Rates of Job Losses Due to Business Contractions, East North Central (ENC) Census Division, 1979–1980

| Business Size | | Business Ownership Status (%)* | | |
	Local	Regional Affiliate	Nonregional Affiliate	Total
Very Small	7.2	5.7	4.5	6.8
Small	9.8	8.1	6.4	8.6
Medium	11.2	17.0	13.7	15.5
Large	11.0	17.0	13.7	15.5
Total	9.1	12.2	9.5	10.5

*Percent of 1976 employment.

TABLE 2.6. Business Survival Rates, East North Central (ENC) Census Division, 1979–1980

| Business Size | | Business Ownership Status (%) | | |
	Local	Regional Affiliate	Nonregional Affiliate	Total
Very Small	76.5	70.5	62.5	74.9
Small	87.6	79.0	72.1	82.0
Medium	91.0	89.8	78.9	87.9
Large	94.5	89.8	78.9	87.9
Total	77.4	73.0	67.7	75.9

Rural businesses generally outperformed urban businesses in the ENC census division.

- Regardless of size, ownership status, or sector, net employment growth was faster in nonmetropolitan counties (Table 2.7).
- Business survival rates were consistently higher in non-metropolitan counties.
- Rural businesses appear to provide more stable employment than urban businesses. The rates of job loss due to closings and contractions were consistently lower in nonmetropolitan counties.
- Absentee owners appear to be more important in rural labor markets. Nonregional affiliates generated a larger share of the net employment growth in nonmetropolitan counties compared to metropolitan counties. Locally owned businesses and very small businesses were more active employers in metropolitan counties.

DISCUSSION OF MAJOR RESULTS

Businesses that are small employers and are in sectors that primarily serve the local economy led the way in generating new jobs in the ENC census division.

Table 2.1 shows that businesses with less than 100 employees were the most active employers. The column labeled "net change" confirms that after subtracting total job losses from total job gains, businesses with less than 20 employees created more net new jobs (approximately 900,000) than any other size category of business. Net employment in the largest businesses, on the other hand, declined by 300,000.

Businesses in the service and trade sectors generated about 1 million of the total 1.4 million net new jobs in the division. The employment change attributed to manufacturing businesses was about 200,000 jobs.

Regionally owned businesses dominated the job generation process. Locally owned businesses generated about 500,000 net new jobs, and corporate affiliates with headquarters in the North Central census region generated about 790,000 (Table 2.1). Corporate affiliates with headquarters outside the region generated only 200,000 of the total 1.4 million net new jobs.

Existing businesses were very important in creating new jobs. Table 2.2 illustrates the overall importance of existing businesses in the job generation process. These firms created about 2.8 million jobs through expansions, about the same as the number created by new firm start-ups. Table 2.3 confirms that business expansions created jobs at a faster rate in every major industrial sector except wholesale and retail trade.

Tables 2.2 and 2.3 also show that jobs were lost primarily because of businesses closing down rather than by existing businesses cutting back on employment. The total loss in the ENC division due to business contractions was 1.6 million jobs compared to 2.5 million jobs lost by firms going out of business.

Business size played an important role in business expansion and retention. The smaller the existing business, the more likely it is to generate jobs through expansion and the less likely it is to lose jobs though contraction. Table 2.3 shows the consistent pattern: The rate of job expansion increases and the rate of contraction decreases as the size of business gets smaller. The expansion rate for very small businesses (28.8 percent) was over three times the rate of expansion by large businesses (8.9 percent). The rate of job loss due to contractions, on the other hand, was only 6.8 percent by small businesses compared to 15.5 percent by large businesses.

The smaller the business, however, the less likely it is to survive. The survival rate (the percentage of 1976 businesses that did not close during

Table 2.7. Sources and Components of Net Employment Change in the East North Central Census Division, Nonmetropolitan County Comparison, 1976–1980

| Item | Share of Net Growth** 1975–1980 | | Rate of Net Growth*** 1976–1980 | | Employment Rate of Change*** Due to: | | | | | | | | Survival Rate*** | |
| | | | | | Start-ups | | Expansions | | Closings | | Business Contractions | | | |
	Met*	Nonmet	Met	Nonmet	Met	Nonmet	Met	Nonmet	Met	Nonmet	Met	Nonmet	Met	Nonmet
Total	100.0	100.0	9.2	14.3	18.1	19.7	18.2	17.8	16.5	14.5	10.5	8.8	75.9	77.7
Business size														
Very small	64.0	50.0	26.9	21.3	26.6	24.5	28.8	23.3	21.8	19.4	6.8	7.2	74.9	76.9
Small	43.0	25.0	16.6	22.5	20.0	23.6	22.9	22.8	17.7	15.7	8.6	8.2	82.0	83.9
Medium	14.0	25.0	4.8	6.9	16.7	14.5	14.2	13.8	15.1	12.8	11.0	8.6	84.3	86.3
Large	-21.0	0.0	-8.8	4.0	10.0	16.5	8.9	7.5	12.2	5.7	15.5	14.5	87.9	92.7
Business Ownership														
Local	35.0	25.0	9.0	8.4	14.0	13.8	17.9	14.3	13.9	13.6	9.1	10.6	77.4	78.2
Regional affiliate	50.0	50.0	10.6	19.7	19.3	21.8	19.4	15.4	15.9	14.8	12.2	9.6	73.0	76.5
Nonregional affiliate	15.0	25.0	6.7	17.3	23.0	24.3	15.8	12.3	22.7	15.2	9.5	7.2	67.0	71.0
Business Sector														
Manufacturing	14.0	25.0	3.3	10.6	14.8	16.5	15.3	16.2	16.0	13.3	10.8	8.9	78.8	79.7
Trade and Service	71.0	50.0	14.0	15.2	21.6	19.7	18.4	17.8	16.9	14.5	9.2	8.8	74.6	76.1
Other	15.0	25.0	8.9	21.5	15.9	22.5	22.8	26.0	16.4	14.6	13.4	12.4	78.0	81.2

*Metropolitan counties are counties that were designated by the U.S. Office of Management and Budget in Standard Metropolitan Statistical Areas (urban population 50,000 and above) in 1980.
**Percent of total.
***Percent of 1976 total.
****Percent of 1976 establishments that did not close, 1976–1980.

the period 1976-1980) decreases and the rate of job loss due to closings increases with smaller businesses. The survival rate of very small businesses was about 75 percent compared to about 88 percent for large businesses. The job loss rate due to closings was 21.8 percent for very small businesses compared to only 12.2 percent for large businesses.

Business ownership is another important factor in retention. The more absentee the ownership, the less likely it is to survive. Locally owned businesses had the highest survival rate (77 percent). The rate was lower for regional affiliates (73 percent) and lowest for affiliates with headquarters outside the North Central census region (67 percent).

Both size and ownership were important factors in business performance.

The smaller the business and the more absentee the ownership, the less likely it is to survive. Tables 2.4, 2.5, and 2.6 show that, as a group, very small, nonregional affiliates had the lowest survival rate (62.5 percent), but the highest rate of job expansion (51.9 percent) and the lowest rate of job contraction (4.5 percent). On the other hand, large, locally owned businesses had the highest survival rate as a group (94.5 percent), a low rate of job expansion (10.0 percent), and a high rate of job contraction compared to most other categories of businesses.

Rural businesses generally outperformed urban businesses in the ENC division. Regardless, of size (except very small businesses), ownership (except locally owned businesses), and sector, net employment growth was faster in nonmetropolitan counties. In addition, business survival rates were generally higher in nonmetropolitan counties, regardless of size, ownership, and industrial sector (Table 2.7).

Existing businesses were about as important in expanding employment in nonmetropolitan counties as they were in metropolitan counties. They expanded employment 17.8 percent in nonmetropolitan counties and 18.2 percent in metropolitan counties.

Absentee owners appear to be more important in rural labor markets. Corporate affiliates generated about 75 percent of the net employment growth in nonmetropolitan counties compared to about 65 percent of the net growth in metropolitan counties (Table 2.7). Very small businesses and locally owned businesses were more active employers in metropolitan counties.

CONCLUSIONS

The analysis of job generation in the ENC census division from 1976 to 1980 suggests that it may be beneficial to balance state and local industrial development programs in a way that recognizes the contribution made by different types of businesses. The following recommendations are based exclusively on the results.

Support business R&E programs that encourage existing businesses to remain and grow in the five-state (ENC) area. Firms that stayed in business were a major source of new jobs. In a sluggish regional economy, existing businesses created more new jobs than business start-ups in almost every major industry. Firms that did not remain in business, on the other hand, were responsible for most of the job losses. More jobs were lost by closing businesses than by businesses that cut back their employment.

Promote small entrepreneurship to create jobs. The analysis documents the significant role of very small businesses–those with fewer than twenty employees–in the regional economy. Very small businesses dominated the process of generating new jobs. They created about twice as many net new jobs as all other businesses combined. Start-ups were very important in the process, but expansions by very small existing businesses created more jobs.

Localize the business ownership structure to promote job security. The ENC study confirms the important role of locally owned businesses in providing stable employment. Local businesses, as a group, had the highest survival rate and the lowest rate of employment loss due to closings. The more absentee the corporate ownership of an affiliate, the less likely it is to survive. Corporate affiliates with headquarters outside the North had the least chance for survival from 1976 to 1980.

Do not underestimate the importance of absentee-owned corporate affiliates in generating new employment, particularly in rural areas, nor overestimate the job security they provide. Corporate affiliates created about twice as many net jobs as locally owned businesses. In rural areas they created about three times as many net new jobs as locally owned businesses. Corporate affiliates, however, tend to have a lower survival rate.

A CAUTIONARY NOTE ABOUT THE ANALYSIS

The analysis has three shortcomings. First, the data derived from Dun and Bradstreet records may not be a reliable source for estimating employment change. Employment change over time can be over- or understated depending on the reporting procedure established by Dun and Bradstreet. Second, the contribution of small businesses may be overstated because establishment size instead of firm size is used in the analysis to define small business. "Business size" refers not to the size of the entire company, but to the size of the corporate affiliate. Small affiliates of large corporations are thus counted as small businesses. Also, the large share of employment growth attributed to small businesses may have been by "default." Big businesses have not been performing very well in the job market in recent years. Consequently, small businesses look good. As

Marc Levenson observed in a recent article in *Dun's Business Month,* "their relative performance owes less to their achievements as entrepreneurs than to the woes of large manufacturers."[9] Third, the results for 1976 to 1980 (a period of expansion) could be entirely different for the most recent period, 1980–1985, (a period of recession, recovery, and expansion). The study obviously needs to be updated. Business failures, primarily very small business failures, have steadily increased since 1979.[10] Recent studies, however, have revealed that very small businesses continually start up and generate new jobs over the business cycle. In Wisconsin, for example, very small business generated most of the net new jobs during periods of both economic expansion and recession.[11]

NOTES

1. David L. Birch, *The Job Generation Process,* (Cambridge, Mass.: MIT Program on Neighborhood and Regional Change, 1979).
2. See James P. Miller, "Nonmetro Job Growth and Locational Change in Manufacturing Firms," RDRR No. 24 (Washington, D.C.: U.S. Dept. of Agriculture, ERS, 1980); and Wisconsin Dept. of Development, Division of Policy Development, Bureau of Research, "The Job Generation Process in Wisconsin, 1969–81, Executive Summary," 1984; Catherine Armington, "Trends in Midwest Business Employment," in *Financing Economic Development in the 1980s,* ed. Norman Walzer and David L. Chicoine (New York: Praeger, 1986), 28.
3. Birch, "The Job Generation Process," 1979.
4. I. J. Smith, "The Effect of External Takeovers on Manufacturing Change in the Northern Region Between 1963 and 1973," *Regional Studies* 13(1): 421–37.
5. Andrew Reamer, "State and Local Policy: Copycat or Custom-fit?" *The Entrepreneurial Economy,* 3(11) May 1985, 6–9.
6. Jane Jacobs, "Why TVA Failed," *New York Review of Books,* 31(8) May 1984, 41–47.
7. James P. Miller, "Nonmetro Job Growth and Locational Change in Manufacturing Firms," RDRR No. 24 (Washington, D.C.: U.S. Dept. of Agriculture, ERS, 1980).
8. David Barkley and Robert Anderson, "Rural Manufacturer's Characteristics and Probability of Plant Closings," *Growth and Change,* 13(1) Jan. 1982, 2–8.
9. Marc Levenson, "Small Business: Myth or Reality," *Dun's Business Month,* Sept. 1985, 30–34.
10. Joseph W. Duncan, "Business Failures Decrease by Nearly 10 Percent in the First Two Months of 1985," *Dun and Bradstreet Looks at Business,* 3(2) Mar./Apr. 1985, 1–4.
11. Wisconsin Dept. of Development, Division of Policy Development, Bureau of Research, "The Job Generation Process in Wisconsin, 1969–81, Executive Summary," 1984.

REFERENCES

Armington, Catherine. "Trends in Midwest Business Employment." In *Financing Economic Development in the 1980s: Issues and Trends,* ed. Norman Walzer and David L. Chicoine. New York: Praeger, 1986.

Barkley, David, and Robert Anderson. "Rural Manufacturer's Characteristics and Probability of Plant Closings." *Growth and Change* 13(1) (Jan. 1982): 2–8.

Birch, David L. "The Job Generation Process." Prepared for MIT Program on Neighborhood and Regional Change, MIT, Cambridge, Mass., 1979, photocopy.

Duncan, Joseph W. "Business Failures Decrease by Nearly 10 Percent in the First Two Months of 1985." *Dun and Bradstreet Looks at Business* 3(2) (Mar./Apr. 1985): 1–4.

Erickson, Rodney. "Corporations, Branch Plants, and Employment Stability in Non-metropolitan Areas." In *Industrial Location and Regional Systems,* ed. John Rees et al. Brooklyn, N.Y.: J. F. Bergin Publishers, 1981, 135–58.

Harris, Candee. "U.S. Establishment and Enterprise Microdata: Database Description." Washington, D.C.: The Brookings Institution, Business Microdata Project, Mar. 1984.

Jacobs, Jane. "Why TVA Failed." *New York Review of Books* 31(8) (May 1984): 41–47.

Levenson, Marc. "Small Business: Myth or Reality." *Dun's Business Month* (Sept. 1985): 30–34.

Miller, James P. "Nonmetro Job Growth and Locational Change in Manufacturing Firms." RDRR No. 24 (Washington, D.C.: U.S. Dept. of Agriculture, ERS, 1980).

Reamer, Andrew. "State and Local Policy: Copycat or Custom-fit?" *The Entrepreneurial Economy* 3(11) (May 1985): 6–9.

Smith, I. J. "The Effect of External Takeovers on Manufacturing Change in the Northern Region Between 1963 and 1973." *Regional Studies* 13(1) 1979: 421–37.

Wisconsin Dept. of Development, Division of Policy Development, Bureau of Research. "The Job Generation Process in Wisconsin, 1969–81." Executive Summary, 1984.

Educational Programs on R&E

3

State Educational/Technical Assistance Programs

DANIEL OTTO, GEORGE MORSE, and ELLEN HAGEY

Many states have recognized the importance of retention and expansion (R&E) activities to their state economies and are developing programs to assist existing industries either directly from state offices or indirectly by helping communities develop effective programs. To better understand the types of programs states have developed and are conducting with existing industries, a survey of state development offices in the United States was conducted during the summer of 1985. Responses were received from forty-four states, and literature was received from several of the nonresponding states. This paper reports the results of that survey, with highlights from successful state programs addressing various dimensions of their R&E efforts. Topics covered in the first part of this chapter include the development of R&E programs and the characteristics of local R&E efforts. In the second part of this chapter, three state-level educational programs are examined in detail.

SURVEY OF STATE DEVELOPMENT OFFICES

State Programs

Surveys were sent to the state department handling economic development in all fifty states, with forty-four states responding.[1] The questionnaire was directed to the state economic development office so the response perhaps more nearly represents that office's familiarity with ongoing programs in the state than a comprehensive listing of programs.

The increased attention paid to the importance of local businesses and industries in recent years has apparently raised the priority of R&E activities as forty of the forty-four states in the survey reported that their state had some type of program to assist communities in their efforts to retain and expand existing business. Resources for these R&E programs appear to be primarily administered at the state level as thirty-two of thirty-five states reported that the assistance is coordinated directly through their offices.

A major function of the state office with regard to R&E appears to be a business visitation program at the community level. Thirty-two out of thirty-five states report making regular community visits. More than half of the state offices make fewer than 500 field visits in a year. States making more than 500 visits per year tend to be larger and more densely populated; they are also states with large manufacturing work forces. A similar pattern is observed when the relationship between the number of visits and the level of urbanization in each state is examined.

Nearly all the states reported that their industrial visitation programs are addressing the multiple objectives of sharing information on various state economic development and marketing programs, attempting to get early warning signs of businesses in danger of closing or relocating, encouraging entrepreneurship, and strengthening local and state economic bases.

Local Programs

The survey also questioned the state offices regarding their awareness of R&E programs run by local community groups. Since state offices may not be fully aware of local R&E efforts, this information may be less than a perfect representation of what is occurring in each state. Only seven of the forty-two states reported that there were no local programs or at least that they were not aware of any operating in their state.

Local visits also appear to have multiple objectives that are similar to those reported for the state level. These visits are designed to keep the channels of communication open between businesses and the local R&E group on issues such as local governmental relation problems, expansion plans, and current economic conditions. They also attempt to provide a liaison to programs and services at the state level, establish a better working climate, and present or arrange management assistance seminars.

The information provided by state offices on the number of communities involved in R&E programs suggests considerable scope for additional state and local activity. Of the nineteen states responding to this question, sixteen, or 84 percent, indicated that less than half the communities in their state had local industrial visitation programs, with the most frequent range being 26–50 percent participation. The fact that one state indicated 76–100 percent of its communities had local industrial visitation programs suggests that some states may have interpreted this question as applying only to the relevant-size communities actively pursuing economic development. Even with this interpretation, the low range of percentages suggests ample opportunity for additional community organization and training activities.

R&E Training

While an overwhelming majority of states indicated that they conducted industrial and business visitation programs from the state level, a minority of the state offices (seventeen of thirty-nine reporting) indicated that they provide training for community groups to conduct their own visitation programs. The states conducting these programs typically have three or fewer full-time employees working in the visitation training program. Although states with all sizes of manufacturing work forces are involved in visitation training programs, the larger states appear to be more active and have invested more resources in these training efforts. Because of this commitment of greater resources, these states were able to conduct more training sessions with individual communities. Only two states reported having completed training sessions for more than fifty communities, with thirty to forty-five communities being the most frequently reported number of training sessions.

The objectives of the training sessions for these local groups were consistent with the overall objectives for the state R&E programs. Based on responses or literature provided with the returned survey, the objectives of these local programs include:

1. increasing community awareness of the importance of industry to the area;
2. improving communities' understanding of the economic development process in order to take advantage of new job creation potential from existing industry;
3. encouraging entrepreneurship;
4. developing a format for communities to use in their plant visits;
5. promoting state programs, such as financing, tax incentives, and training opportunities; and
6. improving skills of local businesses in specific areas, such as management and computer usage.

Not all states listed such comprehensive training objectives. In fact, most were oriented toward providing information and promoting industrial visits. Although few of the respondents provided copies of their training materials, many of the states appeared to be conducting a wide variety of training services. Based on survey results, twenty-one of the forty-two states (50 percent) report working on business management training seminars, twenty-five of forty-two states (59.5 percent) were involved in labor training programs, twelve of forty-two states (28.6

percent) were involved in area-wide labor-management committees, and twenty-seven of forty-two states (64.3 percent) were involved in local economic strategic planning.

The degree of urbanization or concentration of total state population in metropolitan areas apparently is strongly related to the size of the manufacturing work force. States with a higher share of total population in metropolitan areas tend to participate more and to have more resources devoted to community visitation training programs and appear to have more fully developed R&E programs than less urbanized states.

Although states have begun to recognize the importance of working with existing industries, most appear not to have allocated sufficient resources to mount adequate, in-depth community R&E programs. Many of the states appear to be spreading the same resources and personnel over several community-based economic development program areas. With large numbers of communities in each state intensely interested in economic development–related activities (including R&E activities), it is difficult to provide adequate attention to training and follow-up. The current low level of participation in visitation programs by communities in most states is another indication of the potential need for additional state and local resources to implement R&E strategies for economic development.

STATE-LEVEL EDUCATIONAL PROGRAMS ON R&E VISITATION PROGRAMS[3]

State-level educational programs on R&E visitation programs have been conducted by state governments, utilities, and universities. In several cases, state educational programs have been partnerships with two or more of these units.

The overall goal of the state-level educational programs is to help communities establish local R&E business visitation programs. The specific goals of the state programs vary somewhat, but in general all attempt to:

1. convince communities to establish R&E as a local economic development priority;
2. help local organizers understand the economic and organizational factors necessary for successful R&E visitation programs;
3. help communities improve their leadership networks and capacities in economic development; and
4. analyze the data from the business visits and suggest tentative recommendations for future action.

Using the data analysis from the visits, a strategic planning process has been emphasized in some states. Others have stressed the need to use the data analysis only as the starting process for a much broader R&E effort aimed at assisting existing businesses. Ohio has emphasized the need for local leaders to be aware of their community's changing economic structure and economic outlook. With this general background on the visitation program, three case studies are now presented (Table 3.1).

The New Jersey R&E Technical Assistance Program

New Jersey's R&E educational program is co-sponsored by the New Jersey Department of Commerce and Economic Development and New Jersey Bell Telephone. In addition to this partnership the Department of Public Administration at Rutgers University has been contracted to prepare the final report for each community. In total the equivalent of three full-time staff members work on the programs.

In New Jersey local leaders receive about two hours of orientation prior to starting the program. Visitors receive one hour of instruction before contacting local firms.

Prior to 1986, twenty-six communities in New Jersey had implemented R&E programs with an additional twelve programs to be completed in 1987. Of the three state programs examined, New Jersey's serves the largest communities in terms of average population and the largest average number of firms per community. The 1986–1987 series of programs were implemented in communities with an average population of 57,082 and an average manufacturing base of fifty-eight firms.

New Jersey's program was the first to recognize the need for state technical assistance with respect to analyzing the survey results and preparing written reports. Final reports for these programs, which are about thirty-five pages in length, describe and illustrate the survey results. Although recommendations based on the survey findings are not written, suggestions for future economic development that are occasionally mentioned by firms during the visits, are included in the report. Twenty-five to thirty copies of the final report are distributed in the community. No summary of the final report is provided.

The New Jersey program also identified the need for developing a series of news releases. News releases were written for five specific stages during the program. One news release, for example, provides information on the goals and objectives of the local R&E program, which helps to motivate volunteers and improves response rates with industries.

The estimated cost per community of the New Jersey program is $18,000, which is paid entirely by the state and New Jersey Bell Telephone.

TABLE 3.1. Characteristics of State Retention and Expansion Technical Assistance Programs 1986–1987

Characteristic	New Jersey	Georgia	Ohio
Principal sponsors	Utilities, state govt.	State govt., utilities	University, state govt.
Training staff			
State staff/FTE	1/1	2/1	2/1
Regional staff (consultants)/FTE	0	0	12/1
Report preparation			
State staff/FTE	3/1	4/1	3/2
Communities			
Completed prior to 1986	26	13	36
Completed in 1986–1987	12	8	14
Average population	57,082	23,500	43,065
Average number of firms visited	58	15	55
Written report includes			
Employment trends and outlook	No	No	Yes
Summary of survey results	Yes	Yes	Yes
Locally written recommendations	Yes	No	Yes
Community involvement			
Written endorsements	No	Yes	Yes
Final report (no. copies)	Yes (30)	Yes (1)	Yes (25)
Summary report (no. copies)	No	Yes (25)	Yes (250)
Community meetings (Avg. attendance)	Yes	Yes	Yes (106)
Training program (hours)			
Local leaders	2	3	12–16
Visitors	1	1	2
Cost for each program	$18,000	$10,500	$9,500
Actual cost paid by community	$0	$0	$500

The Georgia R&E Technical Assistance Program

In Georgia, the Community Development Department at the Georgia Power Company and the State Department of Community Affairs cosponsor the state's technical assistance program for starting R&E visitation programs. Although the Georgia Power Company developed the program in 1984, the Georgia Department of Community Affairs has administered it since 1985. Two staff members implement the program across the state. However, only one of the employees is full-time. Three additional staff members help prepare the final reports and summaries. In total, the equivalent of two full-time staff people work on the state's technical assistance program.

The goals of technical assistance programs are to help communities organize R&E visitation programs and to use the survey results to correct local problems. Local leaders receive three hours of orientation for the program. Visitors receive one hour of training prior to their visits.

To date, the Georgia program has helped thirteen communities implement R&E programs, with another eight having completed their programs during 1987. The average population of the completed programs is 23,500 persons, with an average of fifteen firms visited.

Written endorsements are required from communities prior to initiation of a program. One copy of the final report is given to the community, along with twenty-five copies of the summary. As in Ohio and New Jersey, the communities hold a public meeting at the end of the project to share the final results and recommendations.

The estimated cost per community is $10,500, which is paid entirely by the state and the power company.

The Ohio R&E Technical Assistance Program

Ohio's technical assistance program for helping communities establish R&E visitation programs is cosponsored by Ohio State University's Cooperative Extension Service and the Ohio Department of Development. The extension service conducts the training programs and applied research with funding and counsel from the Ohio Department of Development. Two OSU staff spend about one full-time equivalent (FTE) running training programs for the local coordinators, consultants, and volunteer visitors. These same two people, plus a research associate and part-time secretary, spend about two FTEs preparing the final reports and summaries for the R&E programs. In addition, twelve regional consultants serve as volunteers, contributing about one FTE.

The local coordinator, R&E consultant, and volunteer visitors spend twelve, sixteen, and two hours, respectively, in training. The coordinator and consultant must complete their orientation about one month prior to the volunteer visitor training. A major component of the Ohio training focuses on the economic outlook of local industries. This is an essential element when designing strategic plans for development.

From 1982 to 1986, the Ohio technical assistance program, run by
Ohio State University, consisted primarily of distributing how-to bulletins
and a slide set. During this period, thirty-six communities completed the
R&E visitation program. Starting in mid-1986, with the establishment of
a partnership between Ohio State University and the Department of
Development, the technical assistance program expanded to include
community training and applied research assistance. During the first year,
four programs were completed and another ten were within two months
of completion. Typically, the Ohio program works with small- to medium-
size communities, serving areas with an average population of 43,065.
The smallest Ohio program covered a population of 10,215, while the
largest had a population of 128,483. The 1986–1987 programs surveyed
an average of fifty-five firms.

As in the other states, local sponsors in Ohio seek broad-based
community involvement in the R&E program. To minimize "turf"
problems, Ohio requires local sponsors to obtain written endorsements
for the local R&E effort prior to its starting.

Ohio's written reports are about sixty pages in length and include an
analysis of local employment trends and the economic outlook of local
industries, as well as the summary of the visitation survey results and the
locally written recommendations. Each community receives 25 copies of
the full report and 250 copies of a popular summary. On the average, 106
community leaders attend the meetings held to announce the survey
findings and recommendations.

Transferability of R&E Visitation Program

The establishment of the fifteen state-level technical assistance
programs (in Arizona, Georgia, Indiana, Iowa, Kansas, Michigan,
Minnesota, New Jersey, North Dakota, Ohio, Pennsylvania, Utah,
Wisconsin, and Wyoming) since 1982 suggests the program indeed has
some transferability. The costs of those state programs range from
$57,000 to $360,000 per year–a relatively minor economic development
expenditure.

An estimated 150 communities have completed the structured R&E
approach (similar to the New Jersey, Georgia, and Ohio programs). No
community appears to be too large or too small to participate. Paid local
staff do not have to be available to conduct a successful local program,
although this is clearly helpful. Communities within a county do not have
to demonstrate the ability to work cooperatively. Besides agreeing to
participate in the program and paying a token fee, community leaders do
not have to demonstrate past economic development achievement.

It appears that the only requirement for transferability is an understanding of the program. The most effective means of selling the program
to new communities is introducing them to leaders from communities
that have already completed the program. In states with established
programs this can be done via visits between communities and, on a

larger scale, day-long conferences featuring local R&E leaders. In states just establishing the program this can be done by sending a delegation to one of the day-long conferences in other states or inviting an experienced local leader to speak. A cost-effective means of sharing the success with other states is to show a videotape documentary followed by a telephone question-and-answer period.

NOTES

1. Daniel Otto collected data from states west of the Mississippi River, and George Morse collected data from states east of the river. The survey results were summarized by Dan Otto.

2. Four of these states have programs based on the New Jersey Bell Telephone program. These are: Wisconsin, Michigan, Georgia, and Pennsylvania. Eight of these states have programs based on the Ohio Cooperative Extension Service model. These are: Pennsylvania, Iowa, Arizona, North Dakota, Indiana, Wyoming, Montana, and Utah. Notice that Pennsylvania uses both systems. Kansas and Minnesota have different approaches to R&E visitation.

3. This section was authored by George Morse and Ellen Hagey as a part of the Council of State Government's bulletin on R&E and is reprinted with permission.

4. Hornadle also outlines a number of educational programs in local economic development conducted by the Cooperative Extension Services. Morse, Favero, Mallet, and Youmans discusses Extension Service program directions.

REFERENCES

Honadle, Beth Walter. "The Role of the Cooperative Extension System in Economic Development." In *Economic Development for Rural Revitalization.* Ames, Ia.: Iowa State University, North Central Regional Center for Rural Development, 1987.

Morse, George W., Phil Favero, James Mallet, and Russ Youmans. "CRD Economic Development Directions in the '80s." Invited paper for the National Community Development Program Conference, Atlanta, Ga., 1982.

Otto, Daniel. "Survey of State Retention and Expansion Programs." Presented at North Central Conference on Business Retention and Expansion, Columbus, Oh., 1985.

4

Steps in Conducting Local Business Visitations

GEORGE MORSE and ELLEN HAGEY

Business visitations are only one phase of a retention and expansion (R&E) program. Other phases include efforts to improve firm efficiency (such as labor training, marketing and management seminars, and technology transfer forums) and programs to promote public relations through the sponsorship of industrial awareness days and media campaigns.

Although R&E programs involve many different subprograms, this chapter discusses the implementation of only one—business visitation. Prior to the discussion, the results of business visitation programs in Ohio are reviewed.

EXAMPLES OF R&E RESULTS

The results of R&E visitation programs can be separated into three broad categories:

1. Developing informed leadership
2. Resolving immediate problems mentioned by firms
3. Designing long-term development strategies for the community's economy

Leadership Development

The most important outcome of the program is the improvement of leadership capacity in the community. The improvements in leadership are based on information; that is, increasing the local leaders' knowledge of their community. The leaders obtain a greater awareness of the economic outlook of the local economy, of the economic development options and tools available to them, and of the realistic limits to local development practices they face. Networks of economic development resource people are a natural result of this improved understanding. The network is created as members of the R&E task force work together to solve immediate problems and to design a strategic plan for development.

Solving Immediate Problems

Some immediate, or short-run, problem-solving efforts in Ohio have included helping a firm work with the city council to have a street light installed at its plant entrance, helping a firm secure an agreement to close a city street if the firm convinced the parent company to expand, developing an evacuation plan in the event of a chemical spill disaster, opening communications between disgruntled firm owners and the school superintendent, working with a firm to prevent the possibility of closure or sale, and helping a firm find a new site within the county.

While many of the immediate issues are minor concerns and relate only to individual firms, success with these smaller matters is tremendously important in helping to build the support needed for long-term strategic planning. Success in solving these smaller problems also strengthens the relationship and improves communication between local leaders and local businesses.

Strategic Planning

As described elsewhere, the R&E business visitation team is a means of developing strategic plans.[1] In fourteen Ohio counties, for example, the sixty-page final reports were based on interviews with an average of fifty-five local firms. The reports reviewed changes in local employment, provided a shift-share analysis to better understand these changes, summarized the economic outlook for six major industries, analyzed the survey findings, and offered recommendations for future economic development. The recommendations ranged from subscribing to a newsletter about new state regulations to hiring a full-time economic development director. These recommendations were developed over a seven-month period and nearly half of them were implemented by communities within two months.

STEPS INVOLVED IN AN R&E VISITATION PROGRAM

Although each community's R&E program differs slightly, this section describes fifteen general steps involved in each Ohio program. The responsibility of progressing to each step rests with the five main players, or groups, in a program. They are:

1. state program consultants;
2. certified R&E consultants;
3. certified R&E coordinators;
4. the R&E task force; and
5. volunteer visitors.

One economist and one program assistant serve as the state program consultants. Each program also has one certified R&E consultant, one certified R&E coordinator, ten to fifteen local leaders on the task force, and at least twenty-five volunteers.

As shown in Figure 4.1, the R&E visitation program is a partnership between the state program consultants at Ohio State University and the local leaders. Each step by the OSU staff depends upon the completion of the preceding step by the local sponsor and vice versa.

Step 1: Selling the Program to Local Leaders

Communities learn about R&E programs through mass media, state conferences, newsletters, and word of mouth. Once a community expresses interest in the program, it may request to have a state program consultant speak to its sponsoring group. The cost is $150 for travel expenses. A less costly alternative is to request a videotape from the state program consultants. The videotape, which can be purchased or borrowed, is the most efficient and informative method of introducing the program. Having viewed the videotape, the sponsoring group should hold a question-and-answer period via teleconference with the state program consultants. In this manner the sponsoring agency learns about the program and asks questions of the state program consultants without paying the cost of hosting guest speakers.

In addition to the videotape, brief fact sheets about the R&E program and a copy of a final report from another community's program are provided to the local group. Community leaders are encouraged to contact communities that have already implemented programs to gather even more information about the program. This reference system is one of the most effective ways to sell the program.[2]

Step 2: Application by the Community

To have a successful local R&E visitation program, local leaders must contribute a considerable amount of time and a wide range of groups must participate. A three-step application procedure is used to ensure that a community is both sufficiently organized and committed to conduct a successful R&E program. The three steps are pre-application, a trip to the university, and final application. Each of these steps serve important functions in helping the local group prepare for their R&E visitation program.

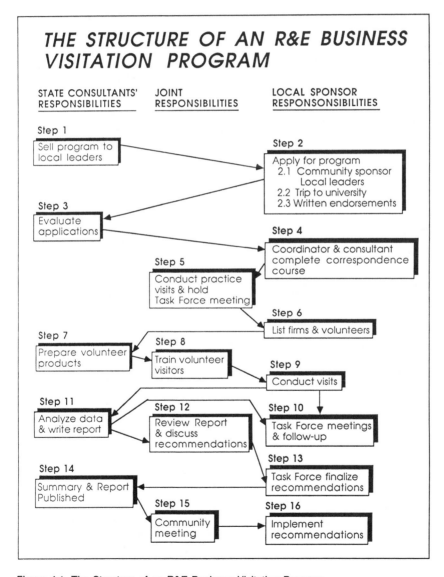

Figure 4.1. The Structure of an R&E Business Visitation Program.

PREAPPLICATION (SELECTION OF COMMUNITY SPONSOR, COOR-
DINATOR, AND CONSULTANT). While sponsors have included community improvement corporations, and city or county governments, each
community is encouraged to include at least one private development
group, such as the chamber of commerce, as a cosponsor. This broad-
based participation should improve the response rate on the visits.

The certified R&E coordinator spends a considerable amount of time
on the R&E visitation program during a three-month period. Estimates
of the total time required by the coordinator range from fifteen to thirty
days. Yet it is an unparalleled opportunity to learn about local firms,
their economic outlooks and development concerns, and the strengths and
weaknesses of the community as a business location. Because of the time
commitment and the potentially long life of the program, it is recommended that the coordinator be a staff member with a local development
group. In small communities, however, this is frequently impossible. In
at least two communities in Ohio, local businessmen have served very
effectively as coordinators. All programs are also encouraged to
designate an assistant coordinator.

The certified R&E consultant is an economic development professional who is very familiar with state and federal development programs.
He or she assists the coordinator in training the volunteer visitors. The
consultant's most important role, however, is helping the coordinator
respond to immediate problems. The consultant reviews and evaluates
each issue noted on each survey and, if necessary, recommends a resource
person in state government who could help resolve the issue. Near the
end of the business visitation program, the consultant also suggests
recommendations for future economic development for the community.
Estimates of the total time required of the consultant range from ten to
fifteen days. Many communities are designating two or three consultants
to work with them.

The R&E task force consists of approximately ten key leaders from
the community's public and private sectors. In Ohio, members of the task
force must include the mayor, a county commissioner, a superintendent
of schools, a banker, a chamber of commerce executive, a Cooperative
Extension Service agent, and two or three other key community leaders.

The group is instrumental in selecting the volunteer visitors, handling
the red-flag issues related to local government, and, most importantly,
writing recommendations for the final report. Each task force member
spends an average of four days on the program.

TRIP TO THE UNIVERSITY (TEST OF INTEREST AND INFORMATION
MEETING). The coordinator, consultant, Cooperative Extension Service
agent, and one or two other key leaders attend this two-hour meeting.
The purpose of the meeting is to clarify any questions concerning the
program. There are three reasons the meeting is held at the university
campus rather than in the community. First, the state program is being

conducted with minimal personnel and this saves at least twelve days per year of staff time. Second, the community is only being charged $500 net fees, and willingness to travel to attend this meeting indicates a high level of commitment on the part of the community leaders. Third, the trip to and from campus often turns into a planning session on the program.

FINAL APPLICATION (SELECTION OF TASK FORCE MEMBERS AND WRITTEN ENDORSEMENTS). To have a successful local program, a wide range of local development groups must participate. To ensure this cooperation, the Ohio program uses an application form that requires each local sponsor to obtain written endorsements from local units of government and other development groups. This requirement forces sponsors to solicit support for the program.

The written endorsements and adoption of the program are then reported to the local media as a means of building awareness and broader support for the program. Further, the endorsements demonstrate to those local leaders participating as either task force members or as volunteers that the program does not reflect a narrow interest group. And finally, the endorsements place a responsibility on the R&E task force to report to each of these groups at the end of the survey to announce the program's accomplishments and findings.

Step 3: Evaluation of Application

Only communities that have demonstrated the ability to complete the application process are accepted into the program. This ensures that only the communities that have decided they really want to complete the program become involved. The competitive nature of the application process provides motivation to go beyond the minimum standards. A sample of the application form and eligibility criteria is provided in Appendix 4.1.

Step 4: Correspondence Course for the Coordinator and Consultant

Few of the certified coordinators and consultants have had experience with the Ohio R&E program. To familiarize themselves with the program, they participate in a correspondence/field experiences course. The training for the consultant differs slightly from that of the coordinator.

The correspondence course involves reading material about R&E, viewing a slide set about the Ohio program, and interviewing experienced coordinators and consultants from other communities. The course assignments, which take about four hours to complete, appear in Appendix 4.2 of this chapter.

Step 5: Practice Visits and First Task Force Meeting

Practice visits are conducted with two firms as part of the training for the coordinator and consultant. Typically, two practice visits are conducted in a given day. Participants include one of the state program consultants, the coordinator, the consultant(s), the county extension agent, and one or two other local leaders. Typically, five or six people go on each practice visit. These practice visits are the official visits for participating firms, however.

The practice visits are critical steps in the orientation of the coordinator and consultants for two reasons. First, some development professionals believe the survey cannot be completed during the interview. These practice visits have changed this opinion in every case. Second, the practice visits give local leaders direct feedback on the reactions of firm representatives to the survey process. While the firm representatives are universally positive to the R&E visit, the practice visits demonstrate this directly.

A meeting with the task force is held after the practice visits. This meeting is essential as it helps to clarify the task force's role in the program. Typically, the meeting takes two hours. Four decisions must be made by the task force at this meeting. First, what are the two local questions they want to add to the R&E survey. Second, who are some other people who should be invited to serve as volunteer visitors? Third, do they want to adopt a policy which reassigns firms when volunteers have not completed the visits within two weeks. Fourth, what dates appear best for the volunteer training?

Step 6: Selecting Volunteer Visitors and Targeting Firms

The task force selects volunteer visitors for the program. The task force is instructed to select local leaders who are actively involved in the community, people who are busy, responsible, and well-respected. Volunteers must also be able to keep confidential all information gathered from the visits. The involvement of local leaders in the program demonstrates the community's appreciation for the local businesses' contribution to the economy and its concern for promoting growth. These people also increase the credibility of the program, final report, and recommendations.

Volunteers should represent both the private and public sectors. Groups that have been represented in previous programs include physicians, lawyers, accountants, manufacturers, school principals and superintendents, realtors, professors, and regional development professionals.

The number of volunteer visitors needed is always half the number of businesses targeted for visitation. The minimum number of volunteer visitors for Ohio programs is twenty-five. Volunteers are paired in teams of two with each team responsible for visiting at least four businesses. Teams are assigned to interview specific businesses.

The firms visited during R&E programs usually include all manufacturing firms and those nonmanufacturing firms with more than fifty employees. If this rule proves impossible to meet because the number of manufacturing firms and large nonmanufacturing firms is quite large, the community uses the results of shift-share analysis to target specific manufacturing and nonmanufacturing sectors to visit.

Step 7: Prepare Volunteer Packets

Each volunteer receives a customized visitor packet. All packets include materials on the R&E program and fact sheets on state and local development programs. The surveys are labelled with the name of the firm, its address and telephone number, and the number of the contact person. Photocopies of the two to five pages from the *U.S. Industrial Outlook* that relate to the industry being visited are included in the packet. Labels with the names and addresses of the two volunteers on the team are put into each packet. The last three items make each volunteer packet unique.

If these packets are ready prior to the training meeting, volunteers can make their appointments with firms immediately after the training. If they are not ready, the two-hour meeting stretches to three or three and one-half hours as the firm assignments and matching is done. Further, there are frequently one- or two-week delays in actually starting the visits.

For a variety of reasons, the preparation of packets has been done poorly by local sponsors in the past. This step is so critical to a smoothly operating program that it is now done at the university.

Step 8: Training Volunteer Visitors

The state program consultants and certified R&E consultant train volunteer visitors for their interviews with local businesses. The training, which requires two and one-half hours, is designed to convince volunteers to participate, to explain their responsibilities, and to provide them with the information, tools, and training necessary for them to complete their interviews.

An agenda for the training sessions is shown in Table 4.1. Each volunteer attends one session; the two sessions are identical and are offered to accommodate the volunteers' schedules. The sponsor of the local program begins the training session by explaining the development of the present program to the volunteers. The sponsor lists the endorsements of local organizations to emphasize the program's broad local support. The sponsor explains the method with which the volunteers were selected, stressing the high standards used in the selection. The sponsor

also explains briefly the purpose or goal of R&E programs, the importance of the business visits, and the necessity of training sessions.

TABLE 4.1. Agenda for Volunteer Training Sessions

Item Person Responsible Time

Introduction	Chairman of Sponsoring	10 minutes
Slide Presentation: "Retention and Expansion: Vanguard for Economic Development"	State Program Consultants	20 minutes
Teleconference and Question-and-Answer Period	State Program Consultants	30 minutes
Break		10 minutes
Review of *U.S. Industrial* *Outlook*	State Program Consultants and R&E Consultant	30 minutes
Review of Survey and Visitation	State Program Consultants and R&E Consultant	20 minutes
Volunteer Teams and Interview Assignments	R&E Coordinator	30 minutes
Total Time:		2½ hours

The sponsor then introduces the consultant who presents the R&E
videotape to ensure that all volunteers understand the program's basic
philosophy and sequence of steps. Following the videotape presentation,
the consultant introduces the state program consultants, one of whom
begins the teleconference question-and-answer period with an experienced
coordinator from another community. The question-and-answer period is
a critical part of the training because it occurs when most volunteers
begin to understand their role in the program but are not as yet
committed to participating. The teleconference helps convince volunteers
to participate because the experienced coordinator often corrects their
misconceptions, reassures their doubts, and increases their enthusiasm.
Volunteers decide at the end of the training session whether or not to
participate. Only a few do not make the commitment.

After the teleconference discussion, the volunteers receive the packet
of information they need to prepare for their interviews. The packets
include R&E literature, surveys, economic outlook summaries, partner
assignments, and firm assignments. The state program consultant explains
effective interviewing techniques for the volunteers to use when they
conduct their visits. He or she also reviews each question in the survey
so that the volunteers understand the purpose of each. The consultant
then explains the importance of the economic outlook summaries for
each business the volunteers visit. The volunteers are encouraged to read

the two- to three-page summaries prior to each interview in order to familiarize themselves with the firm. Finally, a question-and-answer period is held.

Step 9: Conducting the Visits

Each team of volunteer visitors schedules its interview with its assigned businesses. Prior to the training sessions, the coordinator sends introductory letters to each targeted firm explaining the program and announcing that a visitation team will be contacting it for an interview. This letter includes a copy of the survey so firms can see what will be covered in the visit.

If the firm has completed the survey when the visitation team arrives for the interview, the team should go through the survey to make sure that the firm has understood the questions and has completed each one. If the firm has not completed the survey or has misplaced it, the team should give the firm representative another survey. The firm representative should always have a survey for reference during the interview.

It is most efficient and effective if one volunteer from the visitation team asks the survey questions while the other records the representative's answers. The volunteers should reassure the representative that answering the questions is voluntary and that he or she may refuse to answer any question. The volunteers should not promise resolution of any issue mentioned during the interview. They can, however, promise that the R&E task force will attempt to resolve all issues.

After the interview, volunteers complete a short form that indicates whether or not there is a need for an immediate follow-up with the firm and lists the grievances or problems the firm is facing. This form helps the coordinator rank the various issues, giving highest priority to red-flag issues that require immediate attention.

Step 10: Task Force Meetings on Follow-up

The task force holds a series of at least three meetings as soon as the surveys are returned. At each meeting copies of the completed surveys are distributed for review and discussion. To protect the confidentiality of the firms, the cover sheet with the firm name is removed and the first two pages of the survey with the firm's products and employment are detached. An identification number is placed on each survey so that the coordinator and consultant can keep track of the information.

The task force is then divided into groups of three people each. Each group reviews three surveys and discusses the issues to be resolved, the agency that should be contacted, and the person who should be responsible for doing the follow-up. When these decisions have been reached, each small group reports back to the full task force.

TABLE 4.2. Topics Covered in R&E Task Force Meeting

Meeting	Week	Topic Covered
1	2	Review firm surveys
		Use teleconference videos on key development program
2	3	Discuss follow-up status
		Review new firm surveys
		Study employment trends
3	4	Discuss follow-up status
		Review new firm surveys
		Study economic outlook of major firms
	5-11	Optional meetings as desired
4	12	Review written report and start development of recommendations
	13	Subcommittee prepares written recommendations
5	14	Review local recommendations and plan community meeting

*Shows number of weeks after visits start that meeting is held.

The coordinator and consultant screen the surveys prior to the review by the task force and those firms with the most urgent concerns are attended to first. For example, several groups look first at the surveys of firms reporting that they are considering moving and/or expanding. In addition to reviewing the surveys, the task force may cover several other topics as shown in Table 4.2. The teleconference series is used in an early meeting to introduce this new delivery system to them (see Chapter 6). The information on employment trends and economic outlook is presented at these early meetings to avoid information overload at later stages (see Chapter 5). The certified R&E consultant, who has knowledge of state development programs and development professionals, is responsible for advising the coordinator on broad issues. This advisory role is the consultant's most important contribution to an R&E program. A local firm, for example, may want to modernize its plant facilities but has been unable to obtain sufficient information about technological options or opportunities. The consultant will be able to contact the state development professionals who can inform the firm about technological innovations. The consultant can also inform the firm about different state development programs that offer discounts, subsidies, or other incentives for adopting new technology.

Step 11: Analyzing the Data

As the surveys are returned, the coordinator removes the cover sheet for confidentiality, then makes a copy of the survey, sends it to the state program consultants. The state program consultants code and enter the data into a dBase III computer program. They analyze the data and write a summary and final report based on the data analysis. The state program consultants also propose tentative recommendations for future economic development based on the findings. These recommendations are organized around the conceptual model presented in Chapter 1. Four major strategies and the survey data related to each strategy are presented. These strategies are:

1. improve the competitiveness of local firms by helping them use state and federal development programs;
2. enhance the attractiveness of the community by improving its quality of life by solving the educational and public service problems identified by the R&E survey;
3. upgrade the attractiveness of the community through expanded labor training and improved labor/management relations; and
4. increase the community's ability to handle structural changes from global and national economic forces through expanded contingency and strategic planning.

Step 12: Review of Report

Once the draft report is completed, it is sent to the local task force. At a two-hour meeting the state program consultant discusses the conceptual model of the R&E program (Chapter 1), reviews highlights from the firm survey, and presents the four strategies and suggested recommendations. This presentation typically requires about one hour.

During the second hour of the meeting, the nominal group process is used to discuss the recommendations and vote on them. After reviewing the list of recommendations, each task force member is given an opportunity to nominate recommendations for the final report. Each nominated recommendation is written on a blackboard or wall easel. If a recommendation is not nominated, it is not discussed further. After those nominated are discussed, each person can vote for five recommendations, ranking them from most important (= 1) to least important (= 5). Each vote is done on separate slips of paper so that the votes can be easily counted and reported to the group.

The final wording on recommendations is seldom determined at this meeting. But the subcommittee that writes the wording has the votes and the discussion as input.

Step 13: Task Force Finalizes Recommendations

The fifth meeting of the task force is used to finalize the recommendations. If any of the task force members cannot attend this meeting, members at the meeting are assigned to review the final recommendations with those absent. This helps to ensure full support when the recommendations are released to the public.

Only those recommendations on which there is broad-based consensus are included in the final report. This reflects the fact that the R&E task force has no budget or formal authority. Inclusion of items that pass by only a majority vote are unlikely to be implemented.

The importance of the final report and recommendations cannot be overstated. First, they represent a tangible outcome of the program and a vehicle for articulating the program's accomplishments. Second, they provide continuity for the program if adopted as a yearly publication. Third, they provide great visibility for the program and community's probusiness attitude. Fourth, and most important, they include data and recommendations applicable and essential for strategic economic planning.

Step 14: Presenting Recommendations during a Community Meeting

To announce the results of the program and the recommendations for economic development based on those results, a banquet or community meeting is held. All task force members, volunteers, and participating firms are invited as well as state development officials, local, regional, and state politicians, mayors, chambers of commerce, community improvement corporations, county commissioners, and any other organization interested in the community's development. Summaries of the final report are distributed.

Step 15: Implementation and Continuation of R&E Efforts

While the banquet or community meeting denotes the end of the business visitation program, it does not denote the end of the community's R&E efforts. Establishing programs on specific concerns noted during the visits is one means of continuing R&E. Conducting a visitation program with another sector, such as services, is another. Holding quarterly forums for local businesses, realtors, and politicians with invited speakers is still another. Strong R&E programs neither die nor dissipate. They simply continue to help local businesses improve their competitive edge.

SUMMARY

Each R&E program functions a little differently; in fact, there is considerable flexibility in the actual implementation of the program. Still, each involves training volunteers, surveying firms, responding to short- and long-term concerns of firms, analyzing data, reviewing the results, and developing long-range recommendations. Also each program requires a partnership among local leaders, the certified R&E consultant and coordinator, and the state program consultants.

NOTES

1. George W. Morse, "Implementing Strategic Economic Planning in Small Communities via Business R&E Programs: A Research Outline" (Columbus, Oh.: Ohio State University, Dept. of Agricultural Economics and Rural Sociology, Dec. 1986).

2. Educational materials for introducing the program are available for a nominal fee from George Morse, Dept. of Agricultural Economics and Rural Sociology, Ohio State University, 2120 Fyffe Road, Columbus, OH, 43210.

3. For the assignments for coordinators and consultants, see George W. Morse and Ellen E. Hagey, *The R&E Handbook: A Reference Manual for Certified R&E Coordinators and Consultants,* 2d ed. (Columbus, Oh.: Ohio State University, Ohio Cooperative Extension Service, 1988).

REFERENCES

Morse, George W., and Ellen E. Hagey. *The R&E Handbook: A Reference Manual for Certified R&E Coordinators and Consultants,* 2d ed. Columbus, Oh.: Ohio State Univ., Ohio Cooperative Extension Service, 1988.

APPENDIX 4.1

Application Form for an R&E Program in Ohio

Date:

1. Name of Community _____

2. Name of Sponsoring Organization _____

3. Certified R&E Coordinator

    Name _____

    Organization _____

    Address _____

    _____

    Telephone (home) _____ (work) _____

4. Certified R&E Consultant

    Name _____

    Organization _____

    Address _____

    _____

    Telephone (home) _____ (work) _____

5. Please enclose resolution of support from the sponsoring organization.

6. Please enclose resolutions of support from other local organizations, such as the city council, county commissioners, community improvement corporations, chambers of commerce, and other development agencies.

7. Please list the members of the R&E Task Force including their occupation address, and telephone numbers. Members should include chamber of commerce executives, mayor, county commissioners, vocational school representative, cooperative extension agent, banker, and other influential leaders.

8. Please indicate the number of businesses you expect to visit. Break down the total into manufacturing businesses and those nonmanufacturing businesses with more than 50 employees.

9. Please indicate the number of volunteer visitors you expect to recruit. The number should be half that of the businesses to visit. Include their names, occupations, addresses, and telephone numbers.

10. Please include your check with the application.

APPLICATION PROCEDURE
OHIO BUSINESS RETENTION AND EXPANSION PROGRAM

The application process involves three main steps:

    1. pre-application;
    2. OSU meeting; and
    3. final application.

The first step is to submit a pre-application form (attached). This form ensures that some community support for the program exists. The second step is to meet with the OSU staff in Columbus. The purpose of this two-hour meeting is to discuss the community's program in detail with local leaders. The last step is to submit a final application form (attached). This step demonstrates the community's commitment to the program.

Attached are the pre-application and final application forms with explanations. Pre-application forms are due _____ for consideration in the series of R&E programs that begin _____. Final application forms are due _____.

There are no forms for the second step of the application process. The meeting in Columbus should be attended by the community's nominated R&E Coordinator, nominated R&E Consultant, Ohio Cooperative Extension Service CNRD Agent, and perhaps one or two other local leaders.

Please send pre-application and final application forms to your local CNRD Agent at your County Cooperative Extension Office.

If you have questions regarding the application process please call Ellen Hagey, R&E Program Consultant, at 614-292-6451.

Revised 3/88

1

PRE-APPLICATION FORM
OHIO BUSINESS RETENTION AND EXPANSION PROGRAM

1. Name of Community _____

2. Name of Sponsoring Organization _____

3. Nominated Certified R&E Coordinator

    Name _____

    Organization _____

    Address _____

    Telephone (work) _____

4. Nominated Assistant Coordinator (optional)

    Name _____

    Organization _____

    Address _____

    Telephone (work) _____

5. Nominated Certified R&E Consultant(s)

    Name _____

    Organization _____

    Address _____

    Telephone (work) _____

6. County CNRD (Community and Natural Resource Development) Agent

    Name_____

    Organization ___Ohio Cooperative Extension Service___

    Address _____

    Telephone (work) _____

    Agent's Role _____(to be determined at OSU meeting)_____

Revised

2

7. Please enclose a resolution of support from the sponsoring organization.

8. Please indicate the number of establishments you intend to visit. The establishments should be divided into two groups: (1) all manufacturing establishments; and (2) those non-manufacturing establishments with 50 or more employees.

      All manufacturing establishments   _____

      All non-manufacturing
      establishments with 50 or
      more employees   _____

9. Please include a check for $200.00 payable to the Ohio State University.

10. Date of pre-application _____

Revised 3/88

COMPLETING THE PRE-APPLICATION FORM

Name of Community
The community can be either a city or county. Most programs have been county-wide.

Sponsoring Organization
The sponsor(s) may be any group that can provide the necessary leadership and support for a successful R&E program. We recommend that the sponsor be a private development group rather than the city or county. This arrangement adds credibility to the program for the business community. If a city or county wishes to be the sponsor, we recommend that it co-sponsor the program with a chamber of commerce, community improvement corporation, or other private development group. The sponsors role is (1) to provide financial support for the program and (2) to provide secretarial support and office space.

Nominated Certified R&E Coordinator
The Certified R&E Coordinator may be any local leader who is well-known and respected within the community. It is helpful, however, if the person works for a chamber of commerce or community improvement corporation. If the Coordinator is a retired executive, the sponsor needs to provide office space and secretarial assistance during the program which runs at least three months.

The Coordinator does not have to be certified prior to submitting the application. The Coordinator is expected to complete the correspondence course after the program has begun.

Nominated Assistant Coordinator (optional)
Naming an Assistant Coordinator is optional but we recommend it for two reasons. First, programs that experience a change in Coordinators are often delayed by that transitional period possibly resulting in a loss of momentum, a low response rate from firms, or dissipating cooperation from volunteers. Second, there are many details that the Coordinator must address (recruiting volunteers, seeking endorsements, organizing meetings, sending correspondence, keeping records, etc.) in this program. An assistant could share this work load.

Nominated Certified R&E Consultant(s)
The Certified R&E Consultant(s) should be an economic development professional familiar with state development programs and personnel. The following groups are excellent sources of R&E Consultants: utility companies; Economic Development Council; small business enterprise centers; Ohio Technology Transfer Organization; regional development districts; joint vocational school business staff; and technical college business staff.

We recommend that communities have more than one consultant for their R&E programs to delegate the work load and to increase the chances that follow-up to the local establishments' concerns is made.

Revised 3/88

CNRD Extension Agent

Since the R&E program is sponsored in part by the Cooperative Extension Service, your local CNRD (Community and Natural Resource Development) Extension Agent is our local representative. The agent's role will be determined at the OSU meeting (second step in this application process). In every program, the agent is a member of the R&E Task Force. Whether the agent will assume other roles, such as volunteer visitor or publicity chairperson, depends largely on the agent's current work load.

Sponsor's Endorsement

The endorsement states that the sponsor will establish an R&E program once its application has been accepted. It also states that it will support the Coordinator with secretarial assistance and office space if necessary.

Number of Establishments to Visit

Use the most recent issue of County Business Patterns for Ohio to determine the number of manufacturing establishments and those non-manufacturing establishments with more than 50 employees you intend to visit. For city-wide programs, use the most recent issue of Harris Industrial Directory.

Visiting all manufacturing firms and only large non-manufacturing firms (with more than 50 employees) is encouraged. The minimum number of businesses to visit is 50 except for those communities with fewer than 50 businesses.

Check

The check is your first of two payments for the R&E program. The second payment is made with the submission of your final application.

Date of Pre-Application

Please record the date you submit this pre-application.

Revised 3/88

FINAL APPLICATION FORM
OHIO BUSINESS RETENTION AND EXPANSION PROGRAM

1. Please explain in a cover letter the reasons why your community wants to implement an R&E program and why it should be accepted in to this program.

2. Please attach resolutions of support for the program from other local organizations besides the sponsor. Such organizations may include city councils, county commissioners, community improvement corporations, chambers of commerce, mayor's office, financial institutions, utilities, schools, local businesses, or other local organizations. Since numerous resolutions of support indicate widespread support for the program, the greater the number of resolutions, the stronger your application.

3. Please attach a listing of R&E Task Force members including their occupations and mailing addresses. Members should include representatives from the following organizations:

    1. chambers of commerce;
    2. mayor's offices;
    3. county commissioners;
    4. vocational schools;
    5. cooperative extension service;
    6. financial institutions;
    7. and other influential leaders.

Typically, a task force has eight to 10 members.

4. Please attach a listing of the volunteer visitors who you have already recruited to participate in the program. The total number of volunteers needed is half the number of firms you intend to visit. Please include the volunteer's name and occupation. It is not necessary to have the total number of volunteers needed at the time of submitting this application. Nonetheless, the names of at least 15 volunteers who have been approached and have agreed to participate should be listed. When recruiting potential volunteers, request their participation in person or during a telephone call; recruiting volunteers with just a letter is usually ineffective.

Try to recruit volunteers who represent both the public and private sectors of the community. Also, people who have volunteered in other community efforts, such as the United Way, may be more dependable than those who have not participated in similar voluntary efforts. Organizations endorsing your R&E program are often excellent sources of volunteers. As you are recruiting your volunteers it may be helpful to point out to them that their involvement in this program will be approximately 10 hours which includes their training.

4. Please include a check for $1,300.00 payable to the Ohio State University.

Revised 3/

APPENDIX 4.2

Training Course Requirements for Certified
R&E Coordinator and Consultant

ASSIGNMENTS FOR COORDINATORS	ASSIGNMENTS FOR CONSULTANTS
1. Read the fact sheet "Business Visitation Programs" and answer questions.	1. Read the fact sheet "Business Visitation Program" and answer questions.
. View the slide set "Retention and Expansion: Vanguard for Development" and answer questions.	2. View the slide set "Retention and Expansion: Vanguard for Development" and answer questions.
. Read "The R&E Partnership" and answer questions.	3. Read "The R&E Partnership" and answer questions.
. Interview two experienced Coordinators using a question form provided.	4. Interview two experienced Coordinators using a question form provided.
. Based on interviews in assignment 4, write a short summary of an R&E success story with the form provided.	5. Based on interviews in assignment 4, write a short summary of an R&E success story with the form provided.
. Conduct practice visits with two local businesses. Afterward, prepare a one-page summary about the industry based on information in the U.S. Industrial Outlook.	6. Read the article "The Role of the Certified R&E Consultant" and answer questions.
. Hold a Task Force Meeting to discuss its role in the program, confidentially, volunteer training, and practice visits.	7. Prepare a list of state and federal resource people to contact during follow-up phase.
. Read the rest of the R&E Handbook and meet with the Consultant to design a work plan.	8. View at least two videotapes from the Economic Development Teleconference Series. Conduct a question-and-answer teleconference with the resource person in the videotape.
	9. Present a 30-minute workshop about the U.S. Industrial Outlook during the volunteer training sessions.

5

The Application of Secondary Information in Business Visitation Programs

GEORGE MORSE

The data gathered from local firms during the business visitation phase of an R&E program provides local leaders with detailed information about their community's business sector. These data are much more meaningful, however, when studied in the context of national and regional economic and demographic changes, common industrial location factors, and the availability of state and federal assistance for economic development. The inclusion of such secondary data in the business visitation phase increases the success of an R&E program. Rather than being studied from a narrow database, the community is studied relative to regional, national, and global trends.

This chapter describes the possible impact secondary information can have on communities with R&E programs. It also explains the importance of releasing this information piecemeal. The beginning of this chapter is based on a survey of thirty-three Ohio business visitation programs. One of the purposes of the survey was to determine the types of secondary information needed to improve R&E programs.

SECONDARY INFORMATION REQUESTED BY COMMUNITIES

In 1984, thirty-three Ohio business visitation programs were surveyed. The results of the survey indicate that communities requested additional information to supplement the primary data they had collected during the business visits.[1] The supplemental or secondary data they requested included:

1. the economic structure of the community;
2. shifts in the community's share of each type of economic activity (shift-share analysis);
3. the economic outlook of the community's firms individually and collectively;
4. the macroeconomic and international trade situation;
5. demographic changes and forecasts;
6. research findings about the factors influencing industrial location;
7. the availability of state development programs; and
8. the strategic planning process for economic development.

THE ECONOMIC STRUCTURE OF THE COMMUNITY

A description of employment by sector and the changes occuring in each sector provide the background information for strategic planning. Tables 5.1 through 5.3 provide examples of the type of data needed.

Table 5.1 shows the changes in employment in the United States, Ohio, and, in this example, Champaign County for major economic sectors. These sectors are listed according to their growth rates nationally. These data are used to help local leaders understand how their local economy has changed relative to the national and state economies. In this case manufacturing employment had grown slightly in contrast to national and state performances. An understanding of the community's place in the national and industrial economies is essential for the development of realistic strategic plans.

Table 5.2 translates the percentage changes for the county into absolute changes. This is important since large relative changes may reflect only small absolute changes. For the county represented, for example, the services sector grew by 5 percent compared to only 3.1 percent in the manufacturing sector. Yet manufacturing added more than twice as many jobs as the service sector owing to differences in their bases.

Table 5.3 presents a countywide profile of the size of local establishments by industry. This information is often used to determine whether or not the R&E visitation program can include all sectors and establishments. Some communities want to use the data to set a minimum size of

TABLE 5.1. Employment Change by Economic Sectors, 1977–1985

Economic Sectors	United States	Ohio	Champaign County
Very Fast Growth*			
Services	56.0%	47.6%	5.0%
Fast Growth			
Transportation	31.5	10.9	38.6
Construction	30.5	9.3	−37.1
Retail Trade	30.2	24.6	9.6
Finance, Insurance	29.7	19.0	5.4
Wholesale Trade	26.5	11.1	8.8
Slow Growth			
Mining	16.7	−4.0	
Slow Decline			
Manufacturing	−1.1	−16.3	3.1
TOTAL EMPLOYMENT	25.3%	9.6%	13.5%

*Industries are listed by their natural growth rates with services being the fastest growing industry and manufacturing being the least.

TABLE 5.2. Employment Changes in Champaign County, Ohio, 1977–1985

Economic Sectors	March 1977	Change 1977–1985	Percent Change
Very Fast Growth*			
Services	909	45	5.0%
Fast Growth			
Transportation	153	59	38.6
Construction	248	−92	−37.1
Retail Trade	1442	139	9.6
Finance, Insurance	240	13	5.4
Wholesale Trade	342	30	8.8
Slow Growth			
Mining	0	0	0
Slow Decline			
Manufacturing	3212	101	3.1
TOTAL EMPLOYMENT	7484	1009	13.5%

*Industries are listed by their natural growth rates with services being the fastest growing industry and manufacturing being the least.

establishment to be visited. On the one hand, excluding small firms from the program is discouraged since the R&E visitation program can frequently assist small firms more than larger ones. On the other hand, excluding large firms from the program could be embarrassing if a community learns about a closure after it is too late to work with the firm.

TABLE 5.3. Guernsey County Establishments by Employment Size, 1985

Economic Sector	Under 20	20–49	50–99	100+	Total	Total Employment 1985
Mining	29	6	1	1	37	1838
Construction	54	3	–	–	57	510
Manufacturing	26	9	6	6	47	296
Transportation, utilities	31	4	1	1	37	2099
Wholesale trade	50	5	2	–	57	2099
Retail trade	197	19	7	–	223	640
Finance, insurance, real estate	49	4	2	–	55	648
Services	237	11	–	2	250	3232
Others	75	1	–	–	76	175
Total	751	62	19	10	842	9,798

Source: County Business Patterns, 1977 and 1985.

These data can be useful in designing specific technical assistance and educational programs for the community. If the local economy, for example, is concentrated in declining industries, technical and educational programs can be designed to help them either diversify into other sectors or develop new products and markets. As another example, if the local economy is composed mostly of small manufacturing firms, efforts may be taken to secure development assistance for small businesses since a large population of small firms indicates either greater growth potential or a greater closure rate.[2]

SHIFT-SHARE ANALYSIS

Shift-share analysis is used to help target firms. The percentage changes shown in Tables 5.1 and 5.2 tell only a portion of the story since the initial levels of employment differ. The shift-share analysis of Champaign County shown in Table 5.4 shows the changes in absolute numbers of jobs owing to three different factors: the national growth component, the industrial mix component, and the regional share component.

TABLE 5.4. Shift-Share Analysis, Champaign County, 1977–1985

Sector		Component		
	Growth	Industrial Mix	Regional Share	Total Change
Services	230	279	−464	45
Transportation	39	10	10	59
Construction	63	13	−168	−92
Retail trade	365	71	−297	139
Wholesale trade	87	4	−61	30
Mining	0	0	0	0
Manufacturing	813	−847	135	101
Total Employment	1,656	−461	−883	312

The **national growth component** measures the potential number of new jobs created owing to national economic trends. The manufacturing sector in Champaign County's economy, for example, could have grown by 813 jobs (see Table 5.4), or eight times the actual growth of 101 jobs.

The **industrial mix component** measures the degree to which the local economy is concentrated in industries that are growing slower or faster than the national average. Each element of the industrial mix is the product of the employment in 1977 in each sector times the difference between the national growth rate for that sector and the national average growth rate for the whole economy. Notice that the national average growth rate is subtracted to bring the industry back to a zero base before adjusting for the actual growth rate in the sector. Thus, the industrial mix component for the manufacturing sector is illustrated in Table 5.5.

In Champaign County the manufacturing firms are generally in industries with declining U.S. employment. Based on the national rates of decline in these industries, one would expect to see a loss of 847 jobs in manufacturing. Likewise, one would expect an additional 279 jobs in the service sector based on the rates of national growth in this sector.

In total, Champaign County's industrial mix component is a negative 461 from 1977 to 1985. This means that the county's economy had 461 fewer jobs than it would have had if it had a structure similar to that of the nation's economy. This net loss from the industrial mix component reflects the very large loss (-847) from the manufacturing sector.

TABLE 5.5. Industrial Mix Component, Champaign County

1977 Employment	*	Sector's National Growth Rate	−	National Average Growth Rate	=	Industrial Mix Component
(manufacturing)						
3212	*	(−1.1	−	25.3)	=	−847
(services)						
909	*	(56.0	−	25.3)	=	279

The **regional share component** determines whether local businesses are growing faster or slower than similar businesses nationally. This component is the product of the 1977 employment in a sector times the difference between the local growth rate and the national growth rate for that sector. Examples of this are shown for manufacturing and services in Table 5.6.

Thus it can be seen from this example that while manufacturing employment declined nationally, it grew in Champaign County. The local gain in manufacturing was 135 jobs, which is larger than the prediction from the industrial mix component. Yet the service sector grew less rapidly than its counterparts elsewhere in the nation. This resulted in 464 fewer jobs than if services had grown at the national average.

Table 5.4 indicates that every sector except transportation and manufacturing had a negative regional share. This indicates that transportation and manufacturing grew more rapidly in Champaign County than they did nationally. The six other sectors, however, did not grow as rapidly as the national growth rate resulting in a net loss of 883 jobs. The loss of these jobs represents what would be expected given the industrial mix of the county.

This analysis cannot explain why local growth in most sectors is slower than the national averages nor why it is faster in transportation and in manufacturing. On the one hand, some economists suggest that this means local firms are less competitive than firms in their industry. It is reasoned that if output per worker increases, firms will become more competitive, enabling them to expand their market share, production, and employment.

TABLE 5.6. Regional Share Component, Champaign County

1977 Employment	*	Sector's Local Growth Rate	−	Sector's National Growth Rate	=	Regional Share Component
(manufacturing)						
813	*	(−3.1	−	1.1)	=	−135
(services)						
909	*	(5.0	−	56.0)	=	−464

On the other hand, a negative regional share component may signal increasing local wage costs relative to other regions, the lack of new cost-reducing technology, less productive workers, or poor management. Since employment data is used, however, the negative component may signal that the local industry has become more efficient in its use of labor relative to output. Thus those firms with positive local competitive shares may, in fact, simply be slower to adjust to the downward national trends in employment. This suggests that a negative industrial mix and a positive regional share component might lead to additional employment reductions as the industry reflects the national picture more accurately.

ECONOMIC OUTLOOK INFORMATION

The *U.S. Industrial Outlook* provides a quick reference about changes occurring in most manufacturing and nonmanufacturing industries. Each summary indicates the changes in demand, supply, and production technology; costs for raw materials, supplies, and labor; market conditions, and competition that directly affect the sector's growth. The economic outlook for each sector is predicted for the next year and for the next five years.

Volunteer visitors are encouraged to read in advance the two- or three-page summary about the business they will visit. Volunteers have reported that reading these summaries increases not only their understanding of the market trends for the business but also their confidence about conducting the interview. Several volunteers have suggested that being familiar with the industry demonstrates to each business the volunteers' interest. With few exceptions, volunteers have felt that the ten to fifteen minutes invested in reading the summaries is well worthwhile.

The final report includes a summary of the outlook for industries with more than one hundred employees as shown in Table 5.7. The task force is asked to use this table to identify the industry in which the next plant will close. They are then encouraged to read the *U.S. Industrial Outlook* summaries on these industries and discuss them.

TABLE 5.7. Economic Outlook for Major Industries, Guernsey County, 1988–1992.

	Percent Change per Year	
Industry	1988	1992
Firms with 100 to 249 Employees		
Crude petroleum & natural gas (131)	4.4	1.5
Misc. plastics prod. (3079)	8.0	3.0
Telephone communications (481)	8.4	4.4
Nursing and personal care (805)	9.5	?
Firms with 250 to 499 employees		
Electric motors and generators (3621)	0	0
Firms with 500 to 900 employees		
Hospitals (806)	9.1	?

Source: *U.S. Industrial Outlook*, 1988

It is important that this review of the *Outlook* information occurs before the full survey results are available. If the task force receives the two sets of data at the same time, the attention focuses almost exclusively on the survey results.

Macroeconomic and International Trade

In many cases changes in macroeconomic and international trade policies have much more impact on local firms than do local economic policies. While communities cannot directly influence national and international policies, they can learn to adapt quickly. While the information from the *U.S. Industrial Outlook* presents macroeconomic trends for individual sectors, it is useful for the task force to examine broader changes.

The task force is encouraged to review the major changes in the national and international economy as they impact on their local economy. As resources for this review, they are encouraged to conduct the following activities:

1. Appoint an ad hoc subcommittee to review and present the article, "Community Economic Development: Forces, Theories, and Policy Options," in *Economic Development for Rural Revitalization* and to make a short presentation at a task force meeting
2. View the videotape (available from OSU) by Ron Shaffer on the same topic
3. View the videotape (available from OSU) by David Birch on small businesses, job creation, innovation, and entrepreneurship
4. Discuss which of these factors is likely to be of greatest importance in the local economy

Demographic Changes

Changes in a community's population composition have important implications for local development strategies. If few young people, for example, are entering the labor market, expanding businesses and attracting new firms becomes even more difficult. Or, as another example, if the number of elderly citizens is increasing rapidly, expanding or attracting service industries for this group becomes quite logical. The establishment of specific services is dependent upon the age composition of a community's population.

Factors Influencing Industrial Location

Most communities implementing R&E programs are interested in not only retaining and expanding existing firms but also attracting new firms. The R&E visitation program strengthens attraction efforts in several ways. First, it builds positive public relations between existing firms and the community. This relationship is revealed when new firms visit with existing firms and discover the area's healthy probusiness attitude. Such an attitude increases the attractiveness of the area as a business location.

Second, the visitation program indicates, from the business community's perspective, those characteristics of the community that make it an excellent location for business. To increase the utility of this information it should be studied along with research findings about the factors influencing industrial location. By combining the information from these primary and secondary sources, the local task force can best decide how to promote its community in order to attract new firms. Also, it can discuss the methods for improving those areas that seem to lessen the locational attractiveness of the community.

State Development Programs

One of the roles of the volunteer visitors during the business visitation phase of an R&E program is to determine what problems the firm is facing with respect to growth. Often the firms are responsive but the volunteers, despite their training, are not familiar with all the state development programs that may help solve a firm's problem. Providing information about these programs to the firm is essential for a successful program.

Communities in Ohio have used four approaches to disseminate information about development programs. First, economic development practitioners (regional or local representatives of state and federal programs, utility development representatives, local government officials) are invited to participate in monthly forums to discuss development programs and issues. Second, fact sheets describing state and federal development programs are distributed to all volunteer visitors. Third, a teleconference series about economic development programs is presented in each community.[4] Fourth, a quarterly newsletter is published by the Ohio State University about R&E programs and new development programs.

Strategic Planning

The data developed during the R&E visitation program cover most, if not all, of the items needed in the environmental scan stage of strategic planning.[5] After the survey data are compiled and presented, the R&E task force discusses its strategic options and writes its recommendations for the final report. Recommendations are both short-term and long-term. This permits the task force to accomplish some goals immediately. Its enthusiasm and commitment to accomplish the remaining long-term goals is encouraged by initial successes.

Timing and Release of Secondary Information

The information discussed above must be disseminated piecemeal to a community. If provided all at once, the information would overload the R&E participants and, consequently, would be used ineffectively. Before each piece of information is presented, the community must recognize the need for it, otherwise the information will be used ineffectively.

Table 5.8 shows the time at which each piece of information should be released during an R&E visitation program. This schedule is based on programs implemented in Ohio. The state consultant presents information about the community's economic structure to the task force at its first meeting and to the volunteer visitors at their training session. The shift-share analysis is presented to the task force at one of two times. For those communities wanting to visit only a sample of firms, they are presented with the shift-share analysis before the business visits begin. The analysis helps communities target those firms they want to visit. For other communities planning to interview all its businesses, the analysis is presented to the task force after the business visits.

TABLE 5.8. Schedule for Releasing Information to an R&E Task Force

Time Released	Item
Task Force Meeting on Practice Visit Day (1 month prior to R&E visits)	Economic Structure of Community Employment Trends
Volunteer Training	Review of above Details on economic outlook for industries to be visited
1st Task Force Meeting (2 weeks after visits start)	Review of Economic Outlook of Major Firms Detailed discussion of outlook for 2 to 4 major industries
2nd Task Force meetings (3 weeks after visits start)	State development programs via teleconference (VCR/CT) Detailed discussion of outlook for 2 to 4 major industries
3rd task force meeting (4 weeks after visits start)	Macroeconomic trends and industrial location factors
4th and 5th task force meeting (10 to 12 weeks after visits start)	Strategic Planning process
Community Meeting	Economic structure of community Employment trends Outlook for Key Industries

The information about the economic outlook of local industries is presented at least four times during the R&E visitation phase. First, it is presented to the task force at its meeting on the practice visit day.

Next at volunteer visitor training sessions, information is presented on the outlook. At that time, each volunteer visitor receives a copy of the economic outlook for the industries he or she will visit.[6] Third, the outlook is reviewed at the first task force meeting with details presented on two to four major industries in the community. During the following task force meeting, two to four additional industries are summarized. In every case, the summaries are presented after the industry has been visited. The information from the summary is then compared and contrasted to that gathered during the visit to determine the extent to which the firm's situation accurately reflects the general outlook for its industry. Fourth, the outlook information for the community's six major industries is summarized and presented in the final report. The task force reviews these summaries as it develops its recommendations for the community's future development.

The other pieces of information are presented to the task force after the visits start. In most cases the materials are presented by slides or overheads accompanied by a taped message or videotape. A discussion via teleconference is held after the videotape with the person appearing on the videotape. This is most useful because it allows viewers to ask questions directly to the person on the tape. It is also a relatively inexpensive method of hosting an invited guest speaker.

While each of the steps in the R&E program contributes to the strategic planning effort, there is little need to outline the process until the R&E task force is fairly well along. Generally, the connections between the R&E program and strategic planning are discussed ex post rather than ex ante.

SUMMARY

The business visitation phase of an R&E program offers a community the opportunity to understand its local economy and to become aware of the feasible options it has to stimulate growth. To fully use the data collected from the visits, local leaders need supplemental information about the structure of the economy, shifts in the community's employment shares, factors influencing industrial location, economic outlooks or forecasts of local businesses, demographic composition, state development programs, and strategic planning. These items need to be presented at the point that local leaders realize the need for such information.

NOTES

1. See George W. Morse, Kathryn Wilson, and Steven I. Gordon, *Local Industry Visitation Programs: Policy Research and Recommendations,* report prepared for the Ohio Labor Management Committee and the Urban Affairs Program, Ohio State University (Columbus, Oh.: Ohio State University, Dept. of Agricultural Economics and Rural

Sociology, Mar. 1985); or as summarized in George W. Morse, John Rohrer, and Sam J. Crawford, *Retention and Expansion Business Visits: A Guide to Effective Local Economic Development Programs,* Bulletin 728 (Columbus, Oh.: Ohio State University, Ohio Cooperative Extension Service, 1985).

2. See Miller's discussion of this in Chapter 2.

3. The material in *Revitalizing Rural America* is presented.

4. See the discussion by Rohrer and Morse in Chapter 6.

5. See George W. Morse, "Implementing Strategic Economic Planning in Small Communities Via Business R&E Programs: A Research Outline" (Columbus, Oh.: Ohio State University, Dept. of Agricultural Economics and Rural Sociology, December 1986).

6. For a discussion of how to conduct this training, see George W. Morse, John Rohrer, and Sam J. Crawford, *Retention and Expansion Business Visits: A Guide to Effective Local Economic Development Programs,* Bulletin 728 (Columbus, Oh.: Ohio State University, Ohio Cooperative Extension Service, 1985).

REFERENCES

Morse, George W. "Implementing Strategic Economic Planning in Small Communiteis via Business R&E Programs: A Research Outline." Columbus, Oh.: Ohio State Univ., Dept. of Agricultural Economic and Rurual Sociology, Dec. 1986.

Morse, George W., John D. Rohrer, and Sam Crawford. *Retention and Expansion Business Visits.* Bulletin 728. Columbus, Oh.: Ohio State Univ., Ohio Cooperative Extension Service, 1985.

Morse, G. W., Kathryn Wilson, and Steven I. Gordon. *Local Industry Visitation Programs: Policy Research and Recommendations.* Columbus, Oh.: Ohio State Univ., Dept. of Agricultural Economics and Rural Sociology, and the Ohio Cooperative Extension Service, 1985.

Shaffer, Ron, and Glen Pulver. "Community Economic Development: Forces, Theories, and Policy Options." In *Economic Development for Rural Revitalization: A Handbook.* Ames, Ia.: Iowa State Univ., North Central Regional Center for Rural Development, Apr. 1987.

6

Economic Development Teleconferencing Series: The VCR/CT Concept

JOHN D. ROHRER and GEORGE MORSE

Economic trends and the benefits and costs of retention and expansion (R&E) visitation programs have been examined. The question that can now be raised is, How can needed information be provided efficiently and effectively to local volunteer teams? The traditional approach is a person-to-person visit by specialists or program managers. Or written information might be sent about various state and federal programs, visitation tips, etc. The first option is expensive and the second is ineffective.

A 1984 survey of existing R&E programs in Ohio found that most volunteer visitation teams had little orientation prior to the business interviews.[1] As a consequence, few visitors were prepared to provide firms with information on state and federal development programs. In a related study, less than one-third of small businesses had any knowledge of the most basic programs available.[2] In view of the objectives of R&E programs, this information is especially important to improve the efficiency of the firm in production and marketing. Respondents indicated a desire for additional information about the basic purpose and availability of the financing programs.[3] In fact, this was their number one priority for technical assistance. In subsequent follow-up visits with local teams, it was clear that visitors feared information overload when presented with the potential of seventy-five different state-federal development programs.

79

As a result of the above conditions, an objective of the orientation became one of supplying only that information necessary for the volunteer team members to become comfortable in sharing basic information on state or federal development programs. Fact sheets on how to contact the appropriate professional or agency could then be left with the local business. Without the local visitation teams, the state agencies would need to more than triple their current staffs just to reach the state's manufacturing firms.

How can the people responsible for the various programs make contact with the large potential audience in an efficient and effective manner? Time is a precious commodity for both the development professional and those serving on visitation teams. The visitation teams often meet at odd hours (e.g., breakfast meetings) and for short periods of time.

The teleconferencing series was developed to answer this challenge.

TYPES OF TELECONFERENCES

Several variations of teleconferencing have been identified in the literature: basic audio conferencing, one-way video conferencing (with two-way audio), and two-way video conferencing (includes two-way audio).[4] Regular telephone service is considered a one-to-one conversation.

Basic audio conferencing allows more than one person per location and more than two locations to be connected in an interactive conversation.[5] All participants can hear and be heard by one another. The use of visual aids is limited to printed materials such as an agenda or handouts circulated before the meeting. A conference telephone set includes one or more microphones and one or more loudspeakers. It may provide an outlet for a connection to a public address system. An important feature in a conference microphone system is "voice-switched loss" used to reduce sound pickup from all microphones other than the one receiving the loudest signal. With a person speaking into a microphone, this feature reduces the transmission of ambient noise and loudspeaker sounds from causing echoes and audio feedback. A microphone is automatically switched on when someone speaks loudly enough to override the incoming system.

One alternative to voice-switching is the use of a push-to-talk control on the microphones. This is used widely in teaching situations. This system may be inappropriate for highly interactive situations or in formal teleconferences as it may decrease the spontaneity of responses. Highly directional, shotgun microphones have long-range sensitivity and are preferable for use in large conferences having a question-and-answer component.

One-way video, two-way audio conferencing utilizes a master site to transmit a television picture to one or many other sites linked by a two-way audio channel. One way of broadcasting such a program is over a cable channel, low-power TV, or the public broadcasting service station with a telephone number for viewers to call to expand the audio interaction from the specific target group to the general viewing public. A second means of using video is via cassette tapes. The video cassette tapes are mailed to the audience. After viewing the videotapes the audience places a telephone call on an amplified telephone.

Two-way video, two-way audio conferencing permits all participants to see and talk with each other from remote locations. The additional production and transmission costs make it the most expensive medium to use. It also requires more production and has additional constraints in that it requires more rigid planning and scheduling than other modes of teleconferencing.

SOCIAL EVALUATIONS OF TELECONFERENCING

The literature on teleconferencing has reported a number of strengths and weaknesses for audio conferencing.[6] Among the strengths of audio conferencing are:

1. Audio meetings are adequate for a number of typical business and research situations. They are particularly satisfactory for communication tasks that stress information exchange and problem solving.
2. Audio conferences permit rapid communication, with less travel. The use of audio only is most useful when meetings are relatively short and held on a regular basis.
3. Audio meetings permit accurate communication. Research has shown that participants feel they are more attentive to what is being said in an audio system than when communication takes place face-to-face.
4. Audio conferences promote controlled participation as each participant must obtain time and/or recognition from the chair for microphones.

Audio conferencing weaknesses are:

1. Audio meetings are not satisfactory for tasks which stress inter-personal communication, such as negotiation or getting to know someone.
2. Audio conferences can create an impersonal, uncooperative communications environment. There is sometimes skepticism concerning content of a message in an audio-only conference.

This can be mitigated to some extent with a follow-up written message. In group-to-group teleconferencing, "we"/"they" tendencies can develop.

3. Audio may be less productive than other media as research shows that audio groups spend about 10 percent less time on task-related discussion than with either video or face-to-face communication.

4. Audio meetings are personally demanding, i.e., they require more control by the chair than in face-to-face meetings.

5. Users typically have negative expectations about audio.

Video conferencing also has a number of strengths and weaknesses. The strengths are:

1. Video meetings are satisfactory for a wide range of typical business communications particularly when communicating complex information.

2. Video communication is more effective than nonvisual media for interpersonal communication. This is particularly true for participants who do not know each other.

3. The visual capabilities of video systems are more important for some types of group communications. This is particularly true for retention of large amounts of data or for information processing.

4. Video meetings contribute to an orderly atmosphere.

5. New users tend to respond positively to video.

6. Video meetings may be more "persuasive" than meetings via other media.

Video conference weaknesses are:

1. Video meetings are not perceived as satisfactory for communicating with strangers or people of different ranks. Research has shown that video systems are only marginally superior to enhanced audio conferences and less than 20 percent of business meetings need to be conducted by video.

2. Video is better than audio for some interpersonal tasks. It usually does not match the quality of face-to-face meetings.

3. Some of the characteristics of video may be perceived as disadvantageous to the users. The personal communication style may be more noticeable and irritating than in face-to-face or audio-only systems.

Extension Education Use of Teleconferencing

The capability for using both videocassette and amplified telephones has been available to extension for more than five years. In Ohio, relatively little use has been made of this technology in continuing education work. In a 1984 study by Usher and Rohrer, it was found less than half the state or district extension specialists participated in an audio conference more than once or twice a year even though nearly two-thirds of district specialists reported traveling more than two hours to meetings one to three times per week. The participation rate in video conferences was even much less at .03 conferences per respondent.[7]

VCR/CT TELECONFERENCING APPROACH

Recall that a key objective of local R&E teams is to provide basic information to firms in state development programs. It became clear that local businesspeople were reluctant to do this unless they felt confident in their knowledge of the programs. Providing written materials only was felt to be inadequate. Most volunteers also need the opportunity to ask questions about the programs.

VCR/CT Teleconferencing

A new approach that combined both video and audio was developed. A prerecorded videocassette is shown at a remote location to the R&E team, followed immediately by a two-way audio-only amplified telephone call with the resource person seen on the videocassette. This permitted the audience to "see" the person via the video with the "live" exchange by telephone. This system is classified as a one-way video conference with two-way audio. This approach is a new combination of previous methods using a videocassette recorder (VCR) and amplified or conference telephone (CT) or VCR/CT.

This VCR/CT captures many of the advantages of both the video and audio systems but is much cheaper than the two-way video.

A general cost figure for transmission of video conferencing varies from $10 to $20 per minute or over $575 per hour per location.[8] This estimate would include only on-line time and not include equipment, facilities, or staff time to plan and produce the teleconference.

It is becoming even more convenient to use the video and amplified phone systems as they become more available in schools, homes, and local government offices. This often avoids the necessity of moving the more bulky video recorder or monitor to the meeting location. Rather, the meeting is usually held where the equipment (sometimes with large projection screens) is available.

Development of VCR/CT Videotapes

A key ingredient to the Economic Development Teleconferencing Series[9] is the development of a videotape of ten to twenty minutes explaining the development program. The Ohio Cooperative Extension Service and the Department of Agricultural Economics and Rural

Sociology provided funds for two pilot tapes to test the concept. One program was produced by the Extension Information Office, and another was completed with a private video production firm. After initial trials and a demonstration, the Ohio Department of Development arranged for a state government agency to produce twelve additional tapes, that include all major departmental programs. These are relatively inexpensive tapes with an interview format.

Critical Question-and-Answer Period

Instant feedback on the application of programs to local situations is an essential part of the orientation. This could be provided with a personal presentation, but such an approach is very expensive and often impractical, if not impossible, for a twenty-minute presentation.

R&E team members must feel comfortable with the basic elements of the program to be able to discuss them on business firm visits. Fact sheets can then serve as a reminder and outline for the discussion during the visit.

Steps to Use VCR/CT Teleconferencing Series

1. Select a federal or state development program on videotape.
2. Arrange a meeting time satisfactory to the visitation team and the resource person on the videotape. Since travel time is eliminated, the resource person may be able to schedule the telephone Q&A session from nearly any telephone, even on busy days when it would otherwise be impossible. Be sure to check on the location and telephone number of the resource person.
3. Schedule the necessary meeting room and equipment—VHS 1/2-inch videocassette player, TV monitor, cassette tape, and amplified telephone or speaker telephone. It is most convenient to have at least one roving microphone with the telephone set to facilitate questions from the audience.
4. The local contact person should preview the videotape, if possible, and prepare several questions with which to begin the Q&A session.
5. Send each member of the R&E team a fact sheet on the program. Ask two or three of the team members to prepare questions for the discussion period.
6. The local contact person shows the videocassette tape to the R&E team. Some groups may want to discuss the tape for a few minutes and formulate some questions.
7. After viewing the videocassette, call the resource person with the loudspeaker telephone. In certain cases, the resource person may initiate the call, but it is much better for the R&E group to determine the exact time and initiate the call. Decide this procedure when making arrangements with the resource person.

If telephone charges are a problem at the meeting room, a telephone credit card could be used.

It is usually wise to call for a "trial run" before the audience arrives to be sure the equipment is operating properly. Check the microphones to be sure they are connected to the proper control switches.

Conducting the Q&A Session

1. Place the telephone call.
2. Introduce the speaker to the R&E team after the speaker is on the telephone. Give a full introduction of the speaker's background, just as if he or she were present.
3. Have R&E team members introduce themselves in turn and give such personal information as vocation and particular interest in R&E. This may take several minutes, but it is worth the time to put the speaker at ease and helps him relate to the local situation.
4. Interrupt if there is need for clarification, checking technical problems, or more volume.
5. Begin the question period with one or two questions. The first might be, "Have there been any changes in the program since the videotape was made?" Remember, the local leader has to serve as the "eyes" for the speaker to catch body language, then relay audience concerns to the speaker.
6. Provide handout materials, fact sheets, or other information on the program presented.
7. Discuss the teleconference and note any changes for improvement for the next meeting.

Plenty of time should be scheduled for live questions and answers. R&E teams are relatively small groups. This is an advantage; in large group meetings individuals are frequently reluctant to ask questions, and there is usually insufficient time. The Q&A session should provide sufficient opportunity for all team members to ask any questions they may have.

Local teams will likely be able to talk to the more experienced and knowledgeable staff members for development programs because inexperienced staff members would generally avoid an intensive Q&A period. Experienced professionals can usually afford the telephone time because travel time is eliminated. The time of day is also less of a problem—the speaker can usually be available for breakfast or evening meetings.

By focusing on one or two specific development programs, the R&E team is more likely to understand these programs. Professionals often assume too much and forget that local leaders do not have daily contact with many of these programs.

EVALUATION OF VCR/CT TELECONFERENCING SERIES

A pilot program for the teleconferencing series was conducted in four Ohio communities during the spring and summer of 1985. Each of the four pilot R&E teams held at least four meetings and conducted three or four teleconferencing sessions. Most teams viewed one program per meeting, but at least one group studied two different programs at a meeting. Each R&E team completed an evaluation questionnaire following each teleconferencing program. An overall evaluation was also conducted in June and July following the four-meeting series. In answer to the question, "How helpful was the teleconferencing series for your local development efforts?", 46 percent answered "very helpful" or five on a five-point scale. Forty percent checked "helpful" and 14 percent felt it was "somewhat helpful." No respondent checked "not helpful" or "not at all helpful".

In response to a questionnaire and in discussions with the R&E teams, the visual quality of the videotape was not deemed to be a critical question. While people are accustomed to high visual quality on commercial television, apparently a highly motivated group watching a short videotape concerning a self-selected topic will tolerate a head and shoulders picture of the speaker. Very little attempt was made to edit mistakes in speech, and it was taped in one "take" with two cameras. This reduced the cost considerably compared to sophisticated shooting with a lot of editing.

The videocassette can be used repeatedly without a loss in quality. All the R&E teams participating in the pilot project planned to keep copies of the videocassettes in the communities for later use. They planned to use them with selected industry leaders and other groups with or without the immediate follow-up by telephone.

Printed materials are useful and can be used to complement the teleconferencing, but they are often out-of-date. The teleconferencing method provides up-to-date information, particularly important for programs such as development financing.

In the small R&E groups, individuals usually felt free to ask any questions, and they were given adequate opportunity to speak. Participants frequently mentioned this as the most important advantage of the teleconference.

The VCR/CT teleconferencing series eliminates the need for a large audience. In small communities, it is very difficult to arrange a meeting on state and federal programs that will attract a group of twenty or more firms. Yet, using the VCR/CT concept it is feasible to hold a session for very small numbers, even for one firm. Since only minimal costs are being imposed on state agency representatives, they are more willing to participate in a meeting with a small number of firms than they would be if they had to travel to the community.

Although several disadvantages can be cited, they are easily overcome. The videotapes will become obsolete and will need updating as programs change. Mitigating this problem is the telephone follow-up, which can be used to relate any program changes. Equipment is also needed, but it is becoming ever more available in most communities. Other research shows that if all costs were equal, people would prefer personal appearances to any electronic media.[10] In most cases, however, the choice is often between printed material and an interactive electronic medium. Given that choice, the teleconferencing method is much preferred.

ECONOMICS OF VCR/CT TELECONFERENCING SERIES

A comparison of the costs of teleconferencing options requires a careful specification of the information delivery systems. In this chapter only systems that allow a group to dialogue with the resource person will be considered. The five systems are:

1.   speaker travels to meeting;
2.   leaders travel to speaker;
3.   audio conferencing;
4.   video (one-way)/audio (two-way) conferencing; and
5.   two-way video and audio conferencing.

Speaker Travels to Meeting

The first traditional option is still widely used. It provides the standard to which other systems will be compared. Local participants can meet the speaker personally and can interpret such factors as body language and demeanor as well as the material presented. Participants can also offer comments directly and have questions answered immediately. As shown in Table 6.1, a typical meeting is estimated to cost $150.[11] If two speakers were invited to a local meeting, the cost per participant would be $15 per person (assuming twenty participants).

Leaders Travel to Speaker

While there are no initial costs to the community or to the agency sending the speaker to a meeting, the total costs per meeting exceed those of the speaker traveling to the meeting. In this case, the cost would be $560 to the community and $36 to the agency.

One of the reasons for the popularity of the traveling speakers is that frequently all of the costs are borne by the agency rather than by the community. Compare the costs to the agency of the traveling speaker versus the traveling leaders. Agencies find it over four times as expensive to send a representative to the community as to have leaders travel to the

TABLE 6.1. Cost of Alternative Interactive Information Systems

	Initial Cost		Cost Per Meeting		Cost Per Participant		Community Served
	To Community Agency	To Agency	To Community Agency	To Agency	20 Persons	100 Persons	Per FTE
Speaker Travels to Meeting	$ 0	$ 0	$ 0	$150	$ 7.50	$150	130
Leaders Travel to Speaker	0	0	560.00	36	29.80	28.36	345
Audio-conferencing	50	32	32	48	4.00	0.80	260
VCR/CT							
With purchased equipment	1,050	800	28	12	2.00	0.40	1,040
With borrowed equipment	0	800	18	12	1.50	0.30	1,040
Two-Way Video/Two-Way Audio	?	?	?	288	14.40	2.88	?

speaker's headquarters. This is despite the much higher opportunity cost of the leaders traveling to the speakers.[12]

Audio Conferencing

Audio conferencing requires the use of an amplified telephone at the local meeting site. Audio conferences can use visuals at the local meeting site with a meeting coordinator who displays the visuals as the speaker talks. After the formal presentation the speaker can answer questions and dialogue with the local leaders. The audio conference has relatively low initial costs. It only requires the community to purchase a $50 amplified telephone and the speaker to prepare $50 worth of visuals. The operational costs are estimated to be $30 for one-hour's telephone time plus $2 toward the amplified telephone. The cost to the agency is slightly higher than when the leaders travel to the speaker ($48) because it takes an additional hour to prepare the visuals for the audio conference. Yet, the total costs are about half of sending a speaker to the community ($4.00 per participant versus $7.50).

VCR/CT Teleconferencing

The VCR/CT option, the focus of this chapter, has already been described. The initial cost to the community depends upon whether or not the local group would need to purchase the television, a videocassette recorder, and the amplified telephone or whether they can use equipment already in place. If these items must be purchased, then there is $10 of additional cost per meeting, assuming the costs are distributed over five years and the equipment is used twenty times per year. The major reduction ($1.50-$2.00 per participant) is a result of the agency representative spending less preparation time.

The distribution of costs between the community and the agency suggests some interesting institutional changes. Many agencies pay the travel expenses of their personnel and do not charge communities for the travel cost or the time value of the speakers. With the VCR/CT teleconferencing system, the community may be expected to cover more of the cost. The total cost per meeting of the VCR/CT teleconferencing is only about one-fourth the cost of sending the speaker ($30 or $40 per meeting versus $150).

Another major advantage of teleconferencing is that each development staff person can work with more communities. It was assumed that only 50 percent of the staff's time can be spent in the field since they must also prepare materials and administer programs. The traveling speaker can handle only 130 communities per year, or slightly over 2.5 per week. If audio conferencing is used, the speaker's time per meeting is cut in half—each staff person can then handle 260 communities.[13] If leaders travel to the speaker, the staff member can meet with 345 communities with the same time commitment.[14]

The big jump in productivity comes with the teleconferencing series. Since the video is already prepared, the speaker need not use any additional time for preparation. Typically, the calls last thirty minutes. Seldom will more than thirty minutes be spent on making the arrangement for the call and in setting up the initial questions and in preparation. This allows each staff member to reach eight times the number of communities (1,040) that could be reached by traveling (130) and four times that of using the local leader's traveling system (345).

As noted above, two-way video and two-way audio is the most expensive per use at $575 per hour per location. With only twenty or even 100 potential participants, the cost for each is too high to be practical. Assuming twenty people per meeting for thirty minutes, it's $288 for on-line costs only. Costs for equipment, facilities, and staff time to plan and produce the conference are too variable at this time to include in the cost table. Likewise, too few communities are equipped to estimate the potential numbers served. As facilities become available and the average costs are lowered, the two-way video program shows great promise for the future.

TABLE 6.2. Annual Savings for VCR/CT Teleconferencing

Community	Distance for Leaders	Savings* per Meeting	Total*** Savings
London*	40	$ 78	$ 468
Mercer	100	122	732
Medina	100	122	732
Wooster**	80	108	461,160[a]
			to
			2,196,000[b]

Assumes borrowed equipment.
*Reduced by $44 ($24 by saving speaker 2 hours and gass cost by $20).
**Cost by $14.
***Assumes 6 times/year.
[a]Assumes 900 communities (70% use 6 programs each).
[b]Assumes all 900 use all 20 programs.

The annual total savings of using the VCR/CT teleconferencing are shown for four pilot communities and projected on a state-wide basis in Table 6.2. In these four communities the savings per year are estimated to be $2,580. The total savings statewide depends on the number of communities that participate and the number of development programs they wish to study. Assuming 70 percent of the 900 communities participate and use an average of six program tapes, the savings would be over $460,000. If all 900 used all twenty tapes, then the savings would exceed $2 million. These funds could support between ten and forty additional professionals working on economic development.

SUMMARY

The task of finding an economical way for training volunteer R&E teams at dispersed locations around Ohio led to a study of various tele-conferencing methods. The advantages and disadvantages from both a social and economic perspective were studied.

A videocassette followed by an amplified telephone conference (VCR/CT) was selected as an economical and satisfactory method to achieve the objective. Four counties were selected to participate in a pilot project to evaluate the VCR/CT concept. The videocassette followed by amplified telephone permits the time and travel savings of prerecorded messages with the advantage of a "live" Q&A telephone session. R&E teams found the teleconferencing method an excellent way to conduct this part of the orientation.

NOTES

1. George W. Morse, Kathryn Wilson, and Steven I. Gordon, Local Industry Visitation Programs: Policy Research and Recommendations, report prepared for the Ohio Labor Management Committee and the Urban Affairs Program, Ohio State University (Columbus, Oh.: Ohio State University, Dept. of Agricultural Economics and Rural Sociology, Mar. 1985), 46-54.
2. Steven I. Gordon, "Ohio's Business Development Needs: Report on a Survey of Ohio Businesses," (Columbus, Oh.: Ohio State University, Dept. of City and Regional Planning, July 1982), 6.
3. Morse, Wilson, and Gordon, *Local Industry Visitation*, 48.
4. Laurie E. Usher and John D. Rohrer, "Teleconferencing and Its Potential for Use by the Ohio Cooperative Extension Service." Prepared for Dept. of Agricultural Education, Ohio State University, May 1984, 26-27.
5. Enhanced audio-conferencing is not discussed here since it requires equipment seldom available in small- or medium-size communities.
6. This review of social evaluation draws from Usher and Rohrer, "Teleconferencing and Its Potential," 13-15, cited from Zagar, 1982.
7. Usher and Rohrer, "Teleconferencing and Its Potential," 25.
8. Herbert Brodie, "Reach Out and See Someone," *High Technology* (August 1983), 54.
9. In the remainder of the paper, the terms "teleconferencing" or "VCR/CT" will refer to the use of the videotape cassette recorder followed by an amplified conference telephone approach.
10. Usher and Rohrer, "Teleconferencing and Its Potential," 12.
11. This assumes eight hours of speaker's time for a meeting located 100 miles from the speaker's office (4 hours of travel, 2 hours at the meeting, one hour preparation, and one hour arranging the meeting). At an assumed value of $12/hr this costs $96. Mileage charges are $40 and meal charges are $15.
12. Opportunity costs are the value of the time or opportunities given up by undertaking on activity, even if no cash outlay is made.
13. The cost to the community assumes four hours of travel time for twenty leaders with their time valued at $12/hour. Mileage is estimated at twenty cents per mile.

14.   Although the actual meeting of an audio-conference is likely to be only one hour, including discussion, the preparation time for each meeting is likely to be greater since the speaker has to review the visuals and materials and must carefully brief the discussion leader. Consequently, three hours of preparation were assumed.

15.   This additional number reflects the assumption that only three hours will be invested in each meeting (1 hour of preparation and two hours in the meeting).

REFERENCES

Brodie, Herbert. "Reach Out and See Someone." *High Technology*. Aug. 1983.

Gordon, Steven I. "Ohio's Business Development Needs: Report on a Survey of Ohio Businesses." Columbus, Oh.: Dept. of City and Regional Planning, Ohio State University, July 1982.

Lazar, Ellen, et al. *The Teleconferencing Handbook*. White Plains, N.Y.: Knowledge Industry Publications, 1982.

Morse, George W., Kathryn Wilson, and Steven I. Gordon. *Local Industry Visitation Programs: Policy Research and Recommendations*. Report prepared for the Ohio Labor Management Committee and the Urban Affairs Program. Columbus, Oh.: Ohio State University, Dept. of Agricultural Economics and Rural Sociology, Mar. 1985.

Usher, Laurie E., and John D. Rohrer. "Teleconferencing and Its Potential for Use by the Ohio Cooperative Extension Service." Paper prepared for Dept. of Agricultural Education, Ohio State University, May 1984.

7

The R&E Final Report and Survey as Learning Tools

GEORGE MORSE, WILLIAM GILLIS, and DANIEL OTTO

Among the distinctive characteristics of the R&E visitation program are the formal questionnaire and the final report. While there are many differences between the informal R&E visitation programs used in the 1960s and 1970s and the more structured program described in this book, the final report is the most distinct and visible difference. This chapter describes the final report and its use as an educational tool and the questionnaire used in Ohio.

THE FINAL REPORT FOR AN R&E VISITATION PROGRAM

The final report is a critical component of a successful R&E visitation program. First, while the immediate concerns of individual firms are handled without the report, the report presents a composite picture of the community's problems and strengths. Second, the written report summarizes the employment trends of the community, its economic outlook by industry, and its survey results and accomplishments. Third, the written report documents the recommendations written by local leaders and the rationale justifying them. Finally, the written report provides a tangible intermediate product from the program that helps a community not only to continue systematic economic development efforts but also to motivate future volunteer efforts.

Without making the local task force responsible for developing recommendations based on the survey findings, thorough study of the aggregate results from the R&E visitation data might never occur. Rather the process requires the task force to study the data and discuss priorities for future economic development directions prior to writing recommendations. Only in a structured R&E program is this study and discussion guaranteed to happen. The format makes it comfortable for local leaders to participate actively, allowing them to focus on the substance of the report rather than the process. The table of contents for the Guernsey County, Ohio, final report is presented in Appendix 7.1 of this chapter.

Introduction

The educational goal of this segment of the final report is to ensure that all local leaders are aware of the structure of the program and the process used in deriving the final recommendations. Since the volunteers who visited the firms are an important aspect of the process, both the names of the volunteers and the firms are listed. Typically the primary motivating factors for participation by the volunteers and firms are public recognition and fear of embarrassment for not contributing to the betterment of the community. Thus, the listing of firms and volunteers serves as a motivational tool. For this tool to be effective, new volunteers must see copies of previous reports and have heard about this listing during their volunteer training.

Employment Trends and Outlook

This section of the report provides local leaders with information on the changes in employment by sector. The factors that influence these changes are analyzed using shift-share analysis. The major educational objective of the shift-share analysis is to help community leaders understand that many of the changes in their local economy are the result of national and international trends. With this understanding, local leaders can focus on factors of a more local nature.

The summary of the economic outlook for several major industries in the community is also used to help local leaders understand the national forces that affect local firms. To reinforce this understanding, each of the task force members is asked to provide a short summary of these industries at one of the task force meetings. Without these presentations at the early task force meetings, this industrial outlook section in the report tends to be ignored. When local leaders receive this section along with the survey findings, they tend to focus only on the survey findings.

Moving from R&E Visits to Jobs

The saying, "There is nothing more practical than a good theory," motivates this section, which covers the conceptual model presented in Chapter 1 of this book. This model is not shared in an abstract form with local leaders until the final report has been written. At this stage in the program, however, the model ratifies the approaches that the leaders have been taking and enables them to review the survey results more easily and more meaningfully. The model is presented in the fourth task force meeting along with specific, related data from the survey.

Survey Results and Follow-up Strategies

After describing the nature of the firms visited, the survey results are presented around each of the four local strategies for action. This focuses the data on questions of policy. As a result of this approach much of the detail in the data remains undiscussed in the report. The full data results are presented in the appendix to the final report.

The data processing, analysis, and writing of this section of the report is performed either by state program consultants or by development professionals outside the community. While the task force is given the chance to review and comment on the findings, the state program consultant is responsible for the way it is written. The final document is printed by the state program consultant to guarantee the integrity of this section.

To ensure that the results are understood, the "draft" of this section is mailed to the local coordinator for distribution to three or four task force members. Afterward, a full task force meeting with the state program consultant is held to review the results. The state program consultant reviews the results and the tentative recommendations he or she has written for the community. The tentative recommendations are presented only briefly to show their connection with the results. The findings, however, are discussed in depth. Common questions addressed are: What does the data say? Is it an accurate picture of the community? If not, why? What needs to be checked further? At later meetings, the task force writes its recommendations, which may or may not be based on the tentative ones.

Accomplishments

Some final reports include a section on current accomplishments. This documents the immediate follow-up provided to local firms during the R&E visitation program. Where it does not violate confidentiality, specific examples are given about the assistance provided to firms.

The purpose of this section is to demonstrate that the program is interested in action, and is not "just another study." Since most programs do, in fact, provide assistance to many firms from the time the visits begin to the time the task force receives the rough draft of the findings, these accomplishments are recorded in this chapter.

It frequently is difficult to convince local groups to develop this chapter. In some cases they keep very poor records of their assistance to firms. In other cases they have not provided as much assistance to individual firms as they should have. In many cases the coordinator either is too busy or lacks the writing skills to develop this chapter. To facilitate the development of this chapter, local leaders are given a copy of the accomplishments from another program to be used as a guide for their own program. (See Appendix 7.2 of this chapter.)

It is helpful to provide this sample to local coordinators about one week after they start the visits. At this point they can see the necessity of developing this information and it is not too late to collect the data and to respond to the requests.

Recommendations

This section is also written by the local coordinator and R&E task force. Generally the state program consultants provide tentative recommendations for the group to consider. The task force, however, reviews these and nominates and votes on those that they want in the final report. This is meant to encourage the task force to adopt only those recommendations that it feels comfortable in supporting. The task force is encouraged to add, delete, or modify the tentative recommendations.

The final recommendations must be written by the task force to ensure that they are implemented. Recommendations written by professionals from outside the community often may fail to consider local values and past efforts; thus, they are inappropriate and ineffective. Yet, even if professionals write recommendations that consider all possible factors and constraints, local leaders will not share the ownership and responsibility if they do not actively participate in the drafting.

The final set of recommendations, as drafted by local leaders, may not meet all professional criteria. Yet, a professionally drafted set of recommendations that includes one that proves to be unacceptable to the community can result in the local leaders ignoring the entire set of recommendations. Further, local authorship ensures that the task force has read and understood each of the tentative recommendations.

The only requirement under this system is that the task force must provide a short rationale, drawn from the survey results and employment trend analysis, to justify its recommendations. If its justification does not logically lead to the recommendations, the state program consultants discuss this with the local leaders.

Appendices

The appendices list the task force members, the volunteers, firms surveyed, the complete set of tables from the survey, and the survey itself.

It sometimes includes the newspaper articles about the project, the letters of endorsement from other local groups, and the advance letters.

Summary Report on R&E Visitation Program

While the full report runs about fifty pages with another twenty pages of appendices, the summary is only six pages long. A copy of the Defiance County Summary is provided in Appendix 7.3. The first four sections of the full report are condensed to slightly more than one page compared to thirty-five pages in the full report. However, the recommendations, with their rationales, are given in full.

This document is distributed widely in the community. Generally, the first step has been to hold a community meeting to report the results and recommendations. All of the participating firms, volunteer visitors, and local officials are invited to participate in this event.

Then a series of follow-up meetings are held with each of the program endorsers giving an in-depth report on the findings and recommendations of most concern to that group.

This very public sharing of the recommendations in written form provides incentives for the local task force to remain committed to their implementation. The task force is composed of individuals who have earned their reputations as achievers. The members are unlikely to risk these reputations by letting this report sit on a shelf.

THE R&E QUESTIONNAIRE

The survey form, or questionnaire, is shown in Appendix 7.4 of this chapter. Typically the survey takes forty-five to sixty minutes to complete during the visit. Since the survey form is mailed out to the firms prior to the firm visit, a few firms will have completed the form ahead of time. Often, however, the firm representative has reviewed the survey form but has not actually filled it out. In some cases, the form has even been lost. Whatever the situation, the volunteers ask to go through the questions orally. Even if the representative has completed the survey, the volunteers review it to make sure that they understand the firm's responses. If the firm representative needs another copy to follow along with, this is provided. One volunteer simply asks each question, while the other records the responses. Respondents are allowed to skip any question they wish, although this seldom happens.

None of the questions require the establishment to reveal sensitive company information. Questions about sales revenues, net or gross profits, or income are not asked. In fact, the practice of mailing the survey to establishments prior to the visit appears to improve their willingness to participate.

The following discussion of the survey form describes how the information contributes to the knowledge of local leaders and prepares them for strategic planning efforts. While the emphasis in the following discussion is on the generalizations that can be drawn from each question, there is growing evidence that individuals learn new concepts more quickly by inductive than by deductive reasoning. The participation in the surveys and discussion of the results of the individual reports help the R&E task force understand the final results.

Cover Sheet. The top sheet of the questionnaire includes an identification number that is repeated on the second and third sheets of the questionnaire. This allows the local program coordinator to separate the cover sheet from the survey form itself upon the return of the form. This protects the confidentiality of the information when it is mailed to the university for data processing and analysis. The cover sheet is on colored paper while the rest of the survey is on white paper as a visual reminder of the need to separate the sheets.

The cover sheet includes the name and address of the establishment, the names of the persons interviewed, and the interviewers.

Question 1. Position in Company of Person Interviewed. While the R&E team always attempts to talk with the highest management official, this is not always possible. Sometimes the establishment representative is changed at the last minute. The recorder never writes down the name of the individual but only his or her position in the company.

Question 2. Multi-unit Establishment. This refers to branch plants or the headquarters of several plants. If a firm falls into one of these categories, the city and state of the headquarters are reported.

Generally locally owned establishments are less likely to close their operations, other things being equal, than are branch plants. Knowledge of the ownership status provides some early warning clues for the community.

Question 3. Year Establishment Started. Note that this refers to the establishment and not the firm or the company. This data can be used to compare the growth from retention and expansion versus the addition of new plants.

Question 4. Major Products or Services. The nature of the firm's products are important in determining future outlook. Firms producing products with increasing demands will have less difficulty in growing than those producing products with declining demand. Further, the impact of new technology and new products on a firm depends on the products currently being produced.

Earlier versions of the survey asked the firm for its standard industrial code (SIC) but very few could provide this, even in the larger firms. Now the coordinator is asked to provide the SIC for each firm, based on a state industrial directory and other sources.

Volunteer visitors are encouraged to read the *U.S. Industrial Outlook* so they understand the different types of products. Due to the importance of the topic, considerable emphasis is put on this issue in the volunteer training session.

Question 5. Location of Sales. This data is useful in determining the amount of income brought into the county by sales beyond county borders. It provides a clue to the scope of the establishment's market and gives some data on the potential for expanding export sales. This data can also be used in regional input-output models to check the validity of regionalization methods.

Question 6. Raw Materials, Supplies, and Services Needed. These are the items used as inputs to the establishment's production of goods and services. This question is used to explore the possibility that some of these might be produced locally. The percentage purchased outside the county gives some clues as to whether it is currently feasible to produce this input locally. Further, the establishments are asked whether they feel that is economically feasible to produce this input locally. While their responses do not constitute a feasibility study, these firms are probably more familiar with the input industry than most local leaders.

Those products that firms indicate might be produced locally are candidates for further investigation and feasibility studies. Some groups simply publish the list of these suggestions and allow firms that might consider going into these product lines to explore the matter further.

Question 7. Current Number of Employees. This refers to the establishment being visited. If the firm has other establishments, regardless of location, this should be recorded separately.

If there are part-time employees, this is also noted. An estimate of the number of full-time equivalents is computed from these two items.

Question 7a. Location of Employees. This question asks for the percentage of employees living in the county's two major cities, the rest of the county, other Ohio counties, and outside Ohio.

Typically, it demonstrates the relatively high amount of cross-commuting. This suggests that countywide, and even regional, economic development efforts are likely to have high impacts.

Question 8a. Employees Five Years Ago. Again, this applies only to the establishment.

Question 8b. Reasons for the Increase in Employment. Only the three main reasons are asked for to encourage the respondent to identify the

major factors. The reasons listed should be specific—something like
growth in market share or growth in the entire market due to specific
factors. It is common for firms to simply restate the fact that their sales
grew or declined rather than to explain why. Knowledge of the factors
that led to growth or decline in sales may help predict future growth or
decline.

Question 8c. Reasons for Decline in Employment. Only the three main
reasons are requested.

Question 9a. Projected Employment in Five Years. Naturally, such a
projection is difficult. Volunteer visitors should ask for a best estimate.
The reasons for this estimated growth or decline are the most important
aspect of this question. These reasons may suggest ways that the R&E
committee can assist the establishment or, in the extreme cases, ways the
committee can prepare for plant closures.

Question 9b. Reasons for the Change in Employment. Only the three
main reasons should be given.

Question 10. Percent Work Force Unionized. This includes all employees
at the establishment.

Question 11. Location of Major Competitors. This question indicates the
degree to which local firms experience local, regional, national, and
international competition. Firms with local competitors will face different
problems in staying current with their industry than will those with
international competitors.

Question 12a. Recruitment of Employees. Data from this question is very
useful both in attraction programs and in solving problems for existing
firms.

   In the follow-up (12b) the volunteers should be careful to indicate
which group of workers the problem refers to.

Question 13. Rating Labor's Attitude and Productivity. Some communities
have poor labor images that stem from past events rather than current
situations. This question can help to correct that. If, however, management rates the work force low on attitude and productivity, it suggests
the need to explore programs that might improve these.

Question 14. Factors Influencing Future Profits. Forces affecting profits
will likely influence size, and even the survival, of a local firm. Question
9 indicates, from the firm's perspective, whether the firm expects to grow,
decline, or remain stable and the reasons for its expectations. Each of
these reasons is related to supply or demand factors.

Question 15a–b. Major Technological Innovations. If there are major technological changes facing the industry, local firms adopting these innovations may be able to expand. However, for those unable to change, simply remaining competitive may prove impossible. Smaller firms sometimes welcome assistance in evaluating the feasibility of new technology. The R&E task force can assist these firms by connecting them with technology transfer organizations. Larger firms that are more fully aware of their options might or might not be able to remain competitive. If not, early warning of impending problems for these firms provides the community the time needed to explore options for saving the plant or finding a replacement.

New technology frequently means less labor per unit of output. While this reduces employment, it increases profits. This might allow the firm to remain in business when it otherwise could not have been competitive.

While the impacts of new technology are varied and complex, it is important to attempt to understand these potential changes.

Question 16. Information about State Programs. While this information is very general, it provides initial clues about the types of additional information requested. R&E programs can first provide overview descriptions of these programs and then explore the more specific needs of each firm. The R&E program can play a critical role in linking firms with state programs.

From a planning perspective this information suggests which areas are worth more detailed planning and exploration. For example, management seminars were the top priority item of many firms. The R&E program local team can and has created local teams of management educators to explore the specific issues about which firms would like additional information.

Question 17. Permission to Share Name with Department of Development. Notice the follow-up question that asks for permission to share this information with the Department of Development. Without this permission, the follow-up assistance is more difficult to provide. But without asking, some groups felt that they were violating the pledge of confidentiality made to their firms.

Question 17a–e. International Trade Questions. These questions were added at the request of the funding agency, the Ohio Department of Development. The questions were viewed as a means of both determining the degree of interest in the department's new international trade program and in marketing this program.

Question 18a–b. Dissatisfaction with State Agencies/Programs. For this information to be useful, the firm needs to identify specific programs and to describe the specific problem or suggested change. With detailed information the R&E task force can serve in an ombudsman role.

Question 18c. Useful State Programs. While firms tend to remember the agencies that they have had problems with much more clearly than those that have done an excellent job in serving them, it seemed unfair to ask for only negative reactions. Furthermore, the positive information can be useful to local developers that wish to reward local or regional offices for outstanding service.

Question 19a–b. Dissatisfaction with Local Services. Twenty-three public and private services are listed to ensure that this concern is not overlooked. Yet to avoid casual expressions of dissatisfaction, the respondent is asked to explain the nature of the problem and to recommend improvement or changes.

Question 20. Expansion Plans of the Firm. Expanding firms can create both opportunities and problems. Increasing output might require additional local suppliers, as well as additional employees. Yet, if the firm is landlocked, it may need to move, either in or out of its community, to expand.

The follow-up questions (20b and 20c) deal with space for expansion and assistance requested from local development groups.

Question 21a–b. Moving Plans of Establishment. Although few firms that have not announced such plans publicly will reveal to the volunteer visitors their plans to move, it does no harm to ask. The reasons for moving given in Question 21b help local leaders understand the factors influencing industrial location in their community.

Question 22. Location Factors. This question helps community leaders learn about existing firms' attitudes on the relative adequacy of thirteen important location factors. While it would be beneficial to know the relative importance of each item in location decisions, this was not included because many of the respondents were not involved in the location decisions and because it would lengthen the questionnaire.

The question starts "Hypothetically" because obviously the current establishment is already in place. But the question is attempting to assess the reactions for businesses identical to the one being visited.

Question 23. Community as Place to Do Business. This question is designed to provide a summary assessment of the community's business climate as a place to do business.

Question 24. Best Features of Community. This information is often used to market the community in attraction efforts.

Question 25. Recommendations for Improvements. Rather than simply asking for the worst features of the community, this question looks for constructive criticism.

Question 26. Specific Concerns or State Programs. Both this question and the previous one are used to draw out those concerns that are of particular importance to the firm.

Questions 27-28. Local Questions. Every community has certain unique concerns related to economic development. Two local questions allow each community to move away from the standard questionnaire to tap businesses' options about current development issues. The local R&E task force decides what questions to put in this spot.

Follow-up Suggestions. This portion of the survey is completed by the volunteers after the interview. The R&E volunteers are encouraged to ride to the firm together to facilitate the discussion on these issues afterwards.

Key Concern and Urgency. The survey instrument does not record the intensity of feeling about the various concerns that a firm representative may raise. To ensure that this is captured, the volunteers are asked to highlight the key concerns of the firm and then to rate their urgency.

Record of Follow-up Actions. This provides a written record of the actions taken in response to firm requests or problems.

SUMMARY AND CONCLUSIONS

The survey, final report, and summary provide educational or learning tools for local leaders who are designing strategies for local economic employment. The learning occurs first with a particular firm, evolving by induction into generalizations. The data, however, are processed, analyzed, and summarized by professionals outside the community to give an aggregate generalized picture. The discussion of the recommendations by the R&E task force pulls together all of the information and encourages the exchange of views between local leaders needed to move knowledge into action.

Without the final written report, local leaders seldom develop an overall picture of their community's economic structure and its outlook. Further, the development of recommendations provides an opportunity for some in-depth discussion on the actions that need to be undertaken locally and the priorities for these efforts.

APPENDIX 7.1

APPENDIX 7.2

.lthough the program's initial stage of visiting local businesses,
~athering information, and writing recommendations for future economic
~evelopment is complete, several accomplishments have already been
~ade. Since the program began, many firms have received information
~hey requested and many of their problems have been addressed.
~dditional accomplishments, especially solutions to longer-range
~roblems, are expected during 1987.

~uring the business visits, firms requested information frequently
~bout various subjects, such as state and federal development programs
~nd marketing strategies. Table 5 presents a summary of the
~nformation that has been provided to firms. More than 38 percent of
~he information provided involved local government services. Nearly 13
~ercent of the information concerned labor training and another 13
~ercent about financing programs. Most (74.2 percent) of the
~ssistance provided was direct rather than through a referral.

~n addition to supplying firms with information, the R&E Committee
~ontacted firms directly to address their problems or concerns and
~ontacted state and local officials for information and consultation
~bout firms' concerns. Table 6 indicates the types of assistance
~rovided through the R&E program. Although more than half of the
~ssistance provided involved supplying information, 16 percent involved
~ontacting the firms directly, and 25 percent required contacting state
~nd local officials.

~o further illustrate the success of the program thus far, several
~olutions and outcomes to specific problems and concerns revealed
~uring the business visits are discussed below. To maintain
~onfidentiality, those firms involved in these examples are not
~entioned by name.

Improving Roadways

~uring the business visitations several firms complained that the main
~oad leading to the Washington Industrial Park was in poor condition.
~his complaint was relayed to the Washington Court House City Council.
~ealizing the importance of adequate roadways to industries, the City
~ouncil decided to have the road repaved. This improvement benefited
~ll the firms, which employ 1,029 people, in the industrial park.

Table 5

TYPE OF INFORMATION PROVIDED TO FIRMS BY R&E COMMITTEE, 198

TYPE OF ASSISTANCE REQUESTED	Type of Assistance Provided DIRECT	REFERRAL
Labor Training	3	1
New State Regulations	2	0
Financing Programs	4	0
Labor/Management Relations	0	2
Management Seminars	0	0
Export Markets	0	0
Marketing Strategies	3	0
Local Government Services	10	2
Other Issues/Topics	1	3
Total Requests	23	8

Table 6

TYPE OF ASSISTANCE PROVIDED TO FIRMS BY R&E COMMITTEE, 1986

TYPE OF ASSISTANCE PROVIDED	FREQUENCY	PERCENT
Sending factsheets to firms	31	52
Contacting firms after the initial interview to address their problems	10	16
Contacting state or federal agencies on the firms' behalf	3	5
Contacting local officials about firms' local concerns and problems	12	20
Other assistance provided	4	7
Total types of assistance	60	100

Assisting with Expansion Plans

During a business visit a firm requested information about the
procedures it needs to follow to expand its facilities. The firm, which
employs 47 people, received information about obtaining a variance from
the Ohio Industrial Relations Committee. The firm has to obtain the
variance before receiving a building permit. The variance has been
granted and construction, which will increase the warehouse and
production areas, is expected to begin this year. It is estimated that
the expansion could create 15 new jobs.

Referring Firms to Professionals

Two local firms, with a combined workforce of 500 employees, had
several questions about the way in which the state was assessing them
for unemployment benefits. To resolve this situation, the R&E Committee
requested state officials to contact the firms to discuss their
questions. Several state officials representing the Office of
Industrial Development in the Ohio Department of Development and the
Labor Bureau provided personal consultation about the issue.

Creating Linkages

One of the goals of the R&E program in Fayette County is to generate
linkages for and among local establishments. From the information
gathered during the visits, the R&E Committee compiled a list of each
establishment's product lines. This information will help match
suppliers with markets not only within the county but also throughout
southwestern Ohio. This information, in fact, has already helped to
establish a linkage between a local manufacturer and a newly-formed
Japanese industry in southwestern Ohio. It is expected that as this
listing of local product lines is distributed to businesses in the
region, more linkages will be created.

Improving the County's Image

From the visits and surveys, the R&E Committee collected information
disputing the misleading view of Fayette County as having poor
labor/management relations. The specific ratios concerning
labor/mangement relations are mentioned with other survey findings in a
previous chapter. In general, the data suggest that a firm, which is
not presently part of a unionized parent company, locating in Fayette
County is unlikely to become unionized while in the county. Moreover,
those unionized firms that have experienced positive labor/management
relations elsewhere will likely have healthy relations in Fayette
County. This information will be used to promote the county as a an
excellent location for new businesses.

APPENDIX 7.3

R&E — The Ohio Business Retention & Expansion Program

SUMMARY

DEFIANCE COUNTY

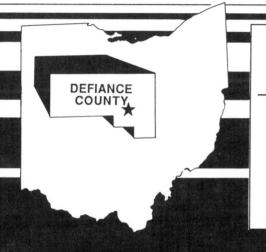

DEFIANCE COUNTY

SUMMARY OF THE 1987 R&E FINAL REPORT

This summary provides highlights from the 1987 Defiance County R&E Program. For a detailed description of the program and its findings, review the Final Report which is available at the offices of the Defiance County Commissioners, Defiance County Cooperative Extension Service, Village of Hicksville, City of Defiance, and the Defiance Area Chamber of Commerce.

OCES

State Sponsors are
The Ohio State University / Ohio Cooperative Extension Service
and The Ohio Department of Development

Local Sponsor is
The Defiance County Community Improvement Corporation

September 1987

THE OHIO
BUSINESS
RETENTION
AND EXPANSION
PROGRAM

DEFIANCE COUNTY'S BUSINESS RETENTION AND EXPANSION PROGRAM

Studies have shown that 70 to 80 percent of all new jobs are created from existing firms rather than from new ones. Consequently, the retention and expansion of existing businesses have become not only practical but also essential economic development strategies for many communities.

Ohio's Business Retention and Expansion (R&E) Program, which is implemented at the county and city level, has one overall goal -- to assist existing businesses in their efforts to compete and expand.

Defiance County's R&E Program officially began during December 1986, with a Business Visitation Program. This program, during which data were gathered from local businesses, is the initial stage in an R&E Program. Before collecting data and visiting firms, 27 volunteer visitors attended a training session in March 1987 to familiarize themselves with the objectives of the program and their responsibilities.

The volunteers visited 44 local businesses during a one-month period. During each visit, the volunteers used a questionnaire to gather information. That information was coded and analyzed at the Ohio State University. Based on the analysis, the Task Force wrote recommendations for future economic development in the county. Those recommendations are presented in this summary.

The success of Defiance County's R&E Business Visitation Program is a result of the leadership and hard work of Mike Schultz, the Certified R&E Coordinator, Tom Suter, the Certified R&E Consultant, and the R&E Task Force members. These members include:

Gary Andres
   Private Industry Council
Michael Brown
   Banker, Industrial Committe,
   Community Improvement Corporation
Darrell Jones
   Defiance County Commissioner
Bill Rohrs
   Defiance County Extension Service
Mike Schultz
   Defiance Area Chamber of Commerce
   Community Improvement Corporation
Tom Suter
   Ohio Technology Transfer Organ-
   ization, Industrial Committee
Tom Wiseman
   Mayor of Defiance, Community Im-
   provement Corporation
Larry Yoder
   Realtor, Industrial Committee

In addition to this local leadership, nine local organizations endorsed the program including:

Defiance Area Chamber of Commerce
Defiance City Council
Defiance County Community Improvement
   Corporation
Defiance County Cooperative Extension
   Service
Defiance County Commissioners
Industrial Development Committee
Maumee Valley Planning Organization
Northwest Ohio Private Industry Coucil
Ohio Bureau of Employment Services

Without this leadership, enthusiasm, and community support this program would not have been possible. The program was sponsored by the Defiance County Community Improvement Corporation, the Ohio State University's Ohio Cooperative Extension Service, and the Ohio Department of Development.

RECOMMENDATIONS

Based on the data analysis of the visits, the R&E Task Force members feel that the potential to improve the economic atmosphere for Defiance County industries does exist, and recommends two major R&E strategies to influence location and investment decisions by firms. These are:

1. The county-wide coordination of economic development activities.

   To accomplish this the Task Force recommends the formation of a county-wide Economic Development Council which would hire and direct a full-time economic development professional. It further recommends that the Council be funded through a partnership of the public and private sectors, and that the Board of Directors should include representatives from a wide base of both the public and private sectors.

2. The review of factors that significantly affect the quality of life for county firms and employees.

   These factors include, but are not limited to, taxes, public utilities, labor-management relations, and a variety of other, already strong county features.

STRATEGY 1

COUNTY-WIDE COORDINATION OF ECONOMIC DEVELOPMENT ACTIVITIES

With many of Defiance County's manufacturing firms in direct competition with international firms and nearly all in competition nationally, it is essential that the recommended Economic Development Council help local firms become more competitive. To become more competitive, firms typically must reduce costs per unit, improve the quality of their products, and/or offer expanded services.

The major sources of cost reduction include increased production through new technology, higher labor productivity, and lower input costs. In Defiance County firms believe that raw material costs will be the most important factor influencing their future profits. Firms rank new products and energy costs third and fourth, respectively, in terms of importance. More than 45 percent of the firms expect major technological innovations to affect their industries during the next five years.

Firms requested information about seven topics, with new state regulations receiving the largest number of requests, followed by labor training and market strategies.

Research shows that many firms, especially small- to medium-sized ones, have a difficult time keeping informed about the large number of public programs available. It is recommended that the Economic Development Council provide information to industry to help firms adapt to new technology, develop new management techniques, and increase productivity.

Another recommended priority of the Economic Development Council would be to develop contingency and strategic plans for local economic development.

With the growth and development of Defiance County increasingly dependent on national and international economic forces and events, the Task Force feels the need for a more solid regional concept of economic development. One-fourth (25.6 percent) of the firms surveyed indicate that more than 50 percent of their employees live within Defiance County but not in the same community as the firm where they work. In addition, 7.7 percent indicate that more than half of their employees live outside Defiance County.

2

While only 31.8 percent of the firms employ 100 or more employees, they account for 89.6 percent of the total work force in the sample. Further, more than half of the firms surveyed are branch plants and employ 89.3 percent of the work force.

For these reasons the Task Force feels that it is important for the Economic Development Council to respond to all industry in the county, to develop contingency plans for plant closings, and to provide strategic economic planning. The Task Force recommends:

▶ I.   Establish a County-wide Economic Development Council

There is a need for a group, with support from the private and public sectors, to focus its total attention on the economic outlook for the county and to suggest alternative contingency and strategic plans.

Teamwork is critical in economic development; yet, turf battles among related development organizations or programs can prevent professionals from collaborating closely, adversely affecting the county. For this reason it is recommended that the Board of Directors include representatives from many existing organizations.

Such a wide base of support shows industry that Defiance County can unite its efforts of retention and expansion, can offer an opportunity to build cooperation between programs, can provide a common ground for learning industry's problems, and can foster industrial development.

▶ II.   Hire a Professional Economic Development Executive

With 64.3 percent of the firms requesting additional information about various state agencies and nearly all

mentioning at least one problem that needed follow-up, it is clear that a professional economic development staff person is needed in Defiance County.

In 45 instances, firms listed raw materials or supplies which they currently purchase outside the county that they believe could be produced within the county. Linkages between supply and demand within the county should be developed by this economic development professional. This person would also organize and manage an industrial center to serve local industry.

▶ III.   Improve Communication and Education Process

Communications are most important to retaining and expanding industry. The visitation program revealed that:

A. More than 45 percent of the firms expect new technology to affect their operations. The Economic Develoment Council needs to provide linkages to the programs, such as the Thomas Edison Program and the Ohio Technology Transfer Organization, that help firms adopt appropriate technology. In addition, half of the firms reported that recruiting skilled labor is a problem. Thus it is important that our local training programs meet these needs.

B. Many state and federal programs have regional or multi-county offices and representatives. In a state with more than 17,000 manufacturing business establishments, service is likely to be quicker and more thorough from these regional offices than through Columbus. With the survey findings revealing a need for information regarding state regulations, labor training programs, and marketing strategies, it is recommended that a factsheet outlining each of the available programs be compiled. It would be distributed to each business establishment.

C. A teleconference videotape series, which describes state and federal programs, should be sponsored. Such a videotape series is available through the Department of Development.

D. A newsletter should be provided to firms with information about state and federal programs and announcements on seminars and meetings for these programs.

IV. Review Critical Forces Affecting Local Economies

The Economic Development Council should review the major changes in the structure of both the national and international economies, and develop an overall strategic plan for future growth in the county.

V. Sponsor Feasibility Studies on New Industry

Based on the data analysis which suggested that some raw materials could be produced or provided in the county, the feasibility of attracting firms should be explored and the nature of the inputs needed should be publicized.

VI. Conduct a Comparative Analysis of Input Costs

According to the firms, raw material costs, wages, new products, energy costs, and taxes will have the largest impact on their profits in the next five years. Yet, data fail to show how Defiance County actually compares to neighboring counties or states on these cost issues. Such a comparison is essential to effectively marketing our strengths, combating partial or incorrect information, and countering future cost-increasing efforts.

VII. Continue the R&E Survey at Two Levels of Detail

There seems to be no reason to repeat the same visitation program in 1988 with the same firms. Since it is desirable to maintain contacts with these firms on an annual basis, it is recommended that a short survey form be used to contact the firms during the next two or three years, repeating the full survey only every four or five years.

●STRATEGY 2

REVIEW OF FACTORS WHICH SIGNIFI-CANTLY AFFECT THE QUALITY OF LIFE FOR COUNTY FIRMS AND THEIR EMPLOYEES

Research and experience indicate that a community's quality of life is an increasingly important factor in location and investment decisions by firms.

The Defiance County R&E survey found generally favorable reactions on the quality of life among the firms visited. In fact, five of the six most highly-ranked location factors are quality-of-life indicators. These are:

Rank	Quality-of-Life Factors
1	Reliability of utilities
2	Schools
3	Access to higher education
4	Public services
5	Recreational opportunities

Firms expect raw material costs to be the major factor influencing their profits during the next five years, followed by wage rates, new products, energy costs, and taxes. In addition, many firms surveyed expressed concern with local services, with a total of 74 complaints recorded. Most of the complaints were about electricity costs, disposal of wastes, street repair, telecommunications, and highways.

4

Thirty percent of the firms believe that a widened Route 24 would have an immediate positive impact on their business or would influence their future plans to expand in the county.

Firms ranked taxes as fifth in terms of their influence on the firms' future profits in Defiance County. Further, local and state taxes were cited as reasons for considering relocation by three and six firms respectively.

Many of the firms expressed dissatisfaction with state agencies and programs, with 59 criticisms cited. The most frequently cited items concerned workers compensation, liability insurance, and tax structure.

Given these findings, the Task Force makes the following recommendations:

I. Review of Taxes on Defiance County Industry

On one hand, state taxes were rated as one of the least favorable location factors, with six of eight firms citing them as one of their reasons for considering moving. On the other hand, 95.2 percent of the firms rated good or fair those services supported by local taxes, with schools ranking as the second highest factor. It is recommended that a comprehensive tax study be initiated to determine the county's relative position to other areas with respect to taxes.

II. Study the Effects of Energy Costs on Industry

It is ironic that the reliability of utilities is the highest-ranking quality-of-life item, while electrial costs are the highest-ranking concern of industry. It is recommended that an independent group be organized to study the effect of utility costs on business and industry, and further, to evaluate

any options which may be available to reduce costs.

III. Review the Need to Improve Telecommunications

Technology and telecommunications are critically important to industries in the future. With 13.6 percent of those interviewed expressing dissatisfaction with local telecommunications, it is felt that an independent group should evaluate the telephone service available throughout the county and suggest ways to modernize it to meet industry's needs in the future.

IV. Highlight the True Labor-Management Relations Picture

Although wages are the second most important influence on firms' future profits, currently more than half (52.3 percent) of the firms indicate that labor costs in Defiance County are good. More than four-fifths rate the attitude (88.1 percent) and productivity (85.8 percent) of their current labor forces as excellent or good. These figures should be utilized when the question of labor-management relations is raised.

V. Publicize the Positive Quality-of-Life Factors

Defiance County received excellent (18.2 percent) or good (70.5 percent) ratings as a place to conduct business by nearly 89 percent of the firms surveyed. Firms said that the people, the size, the business environment, local services, and the work ethic in the county are its best features. About 82 percent rate schools as excellent or good while 66 percent rate recreational activities the same. It is recommended that these features be publicized and used in future industrial attraction efforts, and that local firms should be informed of local services.

APPENDIX 7.4

R&E BUSINESS VISITATION PROGRAM

QUESTIONNAIRE COVER SHEET

Firm ID: _____

Firm:_____

Address:_____

_____

Name and title of person to be interviewed:_____

_____

Names of volunteer visitors:_____

_____

Revised 5/88

Community_____

R&E BUSINESS VISITATION SURVEY

Firm ID_____
Date_____

1.   Position of the person being interviewed:

     1. Owner
     2. Chief executive officer/president
     3. Plant manager
     4. Personnel officer
     5. Other (specify) _____

2.a. Is your establishment part of a multi-unit firm?

     1. Yes
     2. No
     3. Not sure

2.b. Where is your company's headquarters located?

     1. This county
     2. In Ohio
     3. Outside Ohio
     4. Abroad
     5. Not sure

3.   What year was this establishment started in this community?

     _____ Year

4.   What are the major products produced or services offered at this
     establishment? (up to four)

     (1)_____
     (2)_____
     (3)_____
     (4)_____

5.   Where do you sell your products or services?

In the county:	_____	percent
In the rest of Ohio:	_____	percent
In the rest of USA:	_____	percent
Outside the USA:	_____	percent

                    Total = 100%

1

Firm ID_____

6.   What are the three most important raw materials, supplies, or services that you use as inputs in your business?

Raw materials, supplies, or services used?	Percent purchased from outside county?	Is it economically feasible for input to be produced within the county?		
(1) _____	_____	Yes	No	Not sure
(2)_____	_____	Yes	No	Not sure
(3)_____	_____	Yes	No	Not sure

7.   How many employees currently work at this establishment?

_____ full-time employees   _____ part-time employees

Please explain "part-time employees" (i.e., 20 employees working 20 hours/week, 50 employees working full-time for six months, etc.)

_____

7.a.   Please indicate where most of your employees live?

City #1_____: _____ percent
City #2_____: _____ percent
The rest of county: _____ percent
Other Ohio counties: _____ percent
Outside Ohio: _____ percent
                                 Total = 100%

8.a.   How many employees worked here five years ago?

_____ full-time employees   _____ part-time employees

Please explain "part-time employees"

_____

8.b.   If the number of employees has increased, what are the three main reasons?

1. technological changes   7. increase in sales
2. improved management   8. renovation/expansion
3. fast growth/increasing demand   9. new products/services
4. more contracts   10. entered new markets
5. business did not exist 5 years ago 11. less subcontracting
6. improved efficiency   12. other _____

2

Firm ID _____

8.c. If the number of employees has decreased, what are the <u>three</u> <u>main</u>
      reasons?

      1. technological changes   7. renovation/expansion
      2. inadequate management   8. government regulation
      3. slow growth/decreasing demand   9. new products/services
      4. increased competition   10. entered new markets
      5. fewer contracts   11. more subcontracting
      6. corporate decisions/policies   12. other _____

9.a. What is the projected employment level in five years?

      _____ full-time employees   _____ part-time employees

      Please explain "part-time employees"

      _____

9.b. If the number of employees is expected to change, what will be the <u>three</u>
      <u>main</u> reasons?

      1. technological changes   7. increase in sales
      2. improved management   8. renovation/expansion
      3. slow growth/decreasing demand   9. new products/services
      4. increased competition   10. entered new markets
      5. corporate decsions/policies   11. more subcontracting
      6. improved efficiency   12. other _____

10.   What percentage of your <u>workforce</u> is unionized? (includes management)

      _____ percent

11.   Where are most of your major competitors located?

      In the county: _____ percent
      In the rest of Ohio: _____ percent
      In the rest of USA: _____ percent
      Outside the USA: _____ percent
                              Total = 100%

3

Firm ID _____

2.a. Does your company have problems recruiting employees in the following groups?

	Yes	No	Not Sure
Unskilled	1	2	3
Semi-skilled	1	2	3
Skilled	1	2	3
Clerical	1	2	3
Professional/management	1	2	3

2.b. If yes, please circle from the items below those that best describe the nature of your recruiting problems.

1. poor work attitudes
2. available labor has low skills
3. high costs to train employees
4. high competition for skilled employees
5. high wage rates for skilled labor
6. skilled labor is reluctant to migrate here
7. other_____

3. Overall, how do you rate your employees with respect to their

	Excellent	Good	Fair	Poor	Very Poor
Attitude toward work	1	2	3	4	5
Productivity	1	2	3	4	5

4. From the list below, which five factors are likely to have a major impact on your establishment's profits during the next five years? Please rank the five factors from 1 to 5 with 1 being most important.

_____ new products
_____ changing consumer tastes
_____ demographics
_____ higher consumer incomes
_____ defense spending
_____ foreign competition
_____ domestic competition
_____ raw material shortages
_____ energy costs

_____ transportation costs
_____ wage rates
_____ raw material costs
_____ new technology making older plants obsolete
_____ financing availability
_____ taxes/government policies
_____ other factors
_____

4

Firm ID _____

15.a. Are there any major technological innovations on the horizon in your
industry that might affect your company? (please circle one)

       1. Yes   (please answer questions 15.b.)
       2. No   (skip to question 16.a.)
       3. Not sure   (skip to question 16.a.)

15.b. If yes, please indicate the category under which these innovations fall
and whether or not you would like more information about them.

Type of Innovation	Would you like more information?		
1. computer technology	Yes	No	Not sure
2. low-cost substitutes	Yes	No	Not sure
3. quality control systems	Yes	No	Not sure
4. routinizing production processes	Yes	No	Not sure
5. robotics	Yes	No	Not sure
6. lasers	Yes	No	Not sure
7. new materials (i.e. alloys, etc.)	Yes	No	Not sure
8. industry-specific innovations	Yes	No	Not sure
9. other (specify) _____	Yes	No	Not sure

16.a.   Would you like additional information concerning the following
subjects? Please rank the top five those circled "YES" in order of
importance from 1 to 5 with 1 being most important.

	Yes	Rank
Labor training	1	_____
New state regulations	1	_____
Financing programs	1	_____
Labor/Management relations	1	_____
Export/Foreign markets	1	_____
Marketing strategies	1	_____
Management seminars	1	_____
Other _____	1	_____

16.b.   Please specify from your answer above the type of information or
program that you would like more information about.

     (1)_____
     (2) _____
     (3) _____
     (4) _____

Firm ID _____

17.   With your permission, we would like to share your answers (only from
      question 17.a. - 17.e.) and your firm name with the Department of
      Development:_____yes _____no

17.a. Is this establishment currently involved in international trade?

                    1. Yes (please go to questions 17.b., 17.c., and 17.e.)
                    2. No (please go to questions 17.d. and 17.e.)

17.b. If yes, what is the nature of your involvement?

                    1. Direct sales outside the USA
                    2. Work through foreign agents/distributors
                    3. Import products and parts

17.c. If yes, which countries are you involved with?

                    1. Western Europe
                    2. Canada
                    3. Middle East
                    4. East Asia
                    5. Latin America
                    6. Eastern Europe and USSR

17.d. If no, are you interested in becoming involved in international trade?

                    1. Yes
                    2. No
                    3. Not sure

17.e. Is your company interested in finding a foreign partner to form a joint
      venture to license/manufacture/market products internationally?

                    1. Yes
                    2. No
                    3. Not sure

6

18.a. Are you dissatisfied with any of the state programs, agencies, or
policies below? (Circle up to four and answer questions 18.b. and 18.c.)

1. Ohio Dept. of Development program
2. Ohio Job Service
3. JTPA (Job Training
   Partnership Act
4. Energy credit program
5. Equal Employment Services
6. Ohio Bureau of Employment
   Services
7. Medicaid
8. Farmers Home Administration
9. PUCO
10. Ohio Department of Health

11. workers compensation
12. liability insurance
13. tax structure
14. OSHA
15. EPA
16. other inspection agencies
17. wage rates
18. Small Business Admin.
19. state welfare programs
20. highway programs
21. other _____

18.b. Please explain the problem you have experienced with those agencies or
programs circled in question 18.a.

(1)_____

(2)_____

(3)_____

(4)_____

18.c. Which state and federal programs (whether or not they appear in the
above listing) have you found useful and would recommend to other firms?

(1)_____

(2)_____

(3)_____

Firm ID _____

9.a. Please scan the list of local services below and circle those with which
you are dissatisfied (up to six). Then answer question 19.b.

1. Airport facilities
2. Access to shipping
3. Access to highway/roadway
4. Adequacy of highway/roadway
5. Ambulance
6. Health care/hospitals
7. Disposal of processed waste
   material
8. Energy resources
9. Fire protection
10. Inspections (plumbing, etc.)

11. Public parking
12. Public transportation
13. Snow removal
14. Street cleaning
15. Street repair
16. Telecommunications
17. Waste water treatment
18. Water supply
19. Natural gas
20. Electricity
21. Other _____

9.b. Please explain the problems you have experienced with these services.

(1)_____

(2)_____

(3)_____

(4)_____

(5)_____

(6)_____

20.a. Is your company considering expanding at this site within the next five
years?

    1. Yes   (please answer questions 20.b., 20.c.)
    2. No   (please skip to question 21)
    3. Not sure   (please skip to question 21)

20.b. Does your company currently own or lease sufficient property to allow
for the expansion, if necessary?

    1. Yes
    2. No
    3. Not sure

Firm ID _____

20.c. From which of the following agencies has your company requested
      assistance with its expansion plans? (up to three)

      1. Local development department
      2. Community improvement corporation
      3. Area chamber of commerce
      4. University's Small Business Center
      5. Mayor's office
      6. Planning agency/department
      7. Other _____
      8. None

21.a. Are you currently considering moving this establishment?

      1. Yes   (please answer questions 21.b, 21.c)
      2. No   (please skip to question 22)
      3. Not sure   (please skip to question 22)

21.b. Why are you considering relocation?

      1. changing market conditions   7. environmental concerns
      2. overcrowded building   8. rigid code enforcement
      3. no land for expansion   9. high local taxes
      4. transportation problems   10. high state taxes
      5. crime/vandalism   11. lease expiration
      6. low work productivity   12. other _____

21.c. Where are you considering relocating the establishment?

      1. elsewhere in the county
      2. elsewhere in Ohio
      3. Midwest   (Ind., Mich., Ill., Wisc., Missouri, Iowa, Minn., N.
                  Dak., S. Dak., Neb., Kan.)
      4. Northeast (Maine, Vermont, New Hamp., Mass., R.I., Conn., N.J.,
                  N.Y. Penn.)
      5. South   (W.V., Virg., Kent., Tenn., N.C., S.C., Georgia, Alab.,
                  Miss., Fla., Ark., Louis., Okl., Texas)
      6. West   (Wash., Mont., Wym., Ore., Idaho, Utah, Col., N. Mex.,
                  Cal., Ariz., Nev., Alaska, Hawaii)
      7. Abroad
      8. Undecided

9

Firm ID _____

22.   Hypothetically, if you were deciding where to locate your business and
      you were considering this community as a possible site, how would you
      rate the community with respect to the following location factors?

	Excellent	Good	Fair	Poor	Very Poor
1. Vocational training	1	2	3	4	5
2. Access to higher educ.	1	2	3	4	5
3. Schools	1	2	3	4	5
4. Recreational opport.	1	2	3	4	5
5. Public services	1	2	3	4	5
6. Reliability of utilities	1	2	3	4	5
7. Labor costs	1	2	3	4	5
8. Transportation costs	1	2	3	4	5
9. Energy costs	1	2	3	4	5
10. Local taxes	1	2	3	4	5
11. State taxes	1	2	3	4	5
12. Land costs	1	2	3	4	5
13. Building costs	1	2	3	4	5

23.   What is your overall opinion of this community as a place to conduct
      business?

      1. Excellent
      2. Good
      3. Fair
      4. Poor
      5. No opinion

24.   What are the best features from the list below, of this community from a
      business and personal point of view? (circle up to four)

      1. good services (fire, health, etc.)
      2. good business environment
      3. community's size
      4. people
      5. excellent location/proximity
      6. scenic area
      7. good housing
      8. land availability
      9. favorable wage rates
      10. abundant labor
      11. good work ethic
      12. cost of living
      13. schools
      14. other (specify) _____

10

25.   What do you recommend to improve the community? (up to four)

      (1)_____
      (2)_____
      (3)_____
      (4)_____

26.   What specific local concerns would you like to see addressed? (These can
      include ones mentioned earlier in the survey.) (up to four)

      (1)_____
      (2)_____
      (3)_____
      (4)_____

27.   Local Question

28.   Local Question

Thank you for your cooperation with this program. The information you have
provided will be analyzed with that from other local businesses to help
stimulate economic development in our community. The results of this program
will be presented within about six months.

FOLLOW-UP SUGGESTIONS

DATE: _____
FIRM ID:_____

Please complete this short form together in your car after the interview.

1. What is the firm representative's <u>key concern</u> or <u>information request</u>?

2. Rank the urgency of scheduling a follow-up meeting with this business. For example, if a firm is considering relocation, closing, or expanding, follow-up by the R&E Coordinator or Consultant is urgent. If, however, the only real need expressed by the firm representative is to receive information about labor training or financing programs, then the urgency is low. Rank the urgency of follow-up from 1 to 5 with 1 being most urgent.

    Urgency of follow-up _____

Please be sure that your answers and comments are written in ink and are legible. Be sure not to discuss the information conveyed during the interview to anyone except your team partner and the Coordinator. Please return the survey to:

RECORD OF FOLLOW-UP ACTION

(This is completed by the Coordinator)

Firm ID:

Date Completed   Follow-up _____

_____   Thank you letter

_____   Information sent to the firm, if requested.

_____   Telephone call to the firm to either supply information
                               or to discuss some of the information conveyed during
                               the interview, if necessary.

_____   Problem cited during interview is conveyed to local or
                               state agency.

OTHER TYPES OF FOLLOW-UP

Date   Type of Follow-up   Person Responsible

13

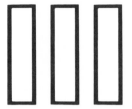

Successful Local R&E
Visitation Programs

8

Success Stories in R&E Business Visitation Programs

GEORGE MORSE, ROBERT MCLAUGHLIN and ELLEN HAGEY

The credibility of an economic development program largely rests on its accomplishments or successes.[1] In economic development, as in most community development programs, there are many ways to measure success. Measuring the number of jobs created from development efforts is relatively simple, whereas measuring the improved cooperation among local organizations or the development of strategic planning is not. This chapter describes the major types of benefits in a Retention and Expansion (R&E) business visitation program. These different types of success are illustrated with examples from local R&E programs in Idaho, Georgia, New Jersey, Ohio, and Wisconsin.

An R&E visitation of businesses is usually the first step in the overall R&E program. Typically, trained volunteers visit local businesses in teams of two to identify and record the firms' concerns or problems affecting their operations, and to determine if technical, labor, managerial, financial, or legal assistance is needed. The volunteers use a questionnaire during the business visit to gather the necessary information about the firm. Following the interview, the team returns the questionnaire to the local R&E coordinator.

The coordinator is the local leader of the program who reviews each questionnaire and decides on the appropriate follow-up action. Local issues are handled locally by the coordinator who contacts organizations or professionals who can help solve a problem mentioned by a firm.

Referring firms to these organizations or professionals or simply sending pertinent information to the firm may suffice.

Some local issues, however, are handled by the R&E task force. The task force is an interdisciplinary group of eight or ten local leaders representing local government, civic organizations, the school system, banks, and other organizations interested in local economic development. The interdisciplinary character of the task force is ideal when members discuss possible solutions to concerns, issues, or problems mentioned by local firms.

Issues of a nonlocal nature may be handled by the R&E consultant. The consultant is an economic development professional who is very familiar with state and federal economic development programs. The consultant's extensive network of development professionals and knowledge of available programs is critically important to successful follow-up work during a program.

After the coordinator reviews each questionnaire, a copy is sent to the state R&E leaders (usually located at a university) where the data are coded and analyzed. The results are sent to the task force, which reviews them along with secondary information describing the community. The task force writes recommendations based on this information.

The R&E visitation program not only yields different types of outcomes, but also does so at different program stages. Some of the successes tend to occur immediately while others take much longer to develop. The short-run impacts of the program include:

1. demonstration by program participants of the community's probusiness attitude;
2. development of a high degree of cooperation between public and private development agencies and leaders;
3. creation of a forum in which sensitive information regarding local businesses' needs or complaints can be addressed effectively yet confidentially; and
4. collection of data regarding the community's strengths and weaknesses as a place in which to do business.

In the long run, the R&E program impacts include:

1. improved understanding among community leaders about the economic outlook of the community;
2. development of a comprehensive strategic plan for encouraging local economic development;
3. implementation of programs that improve the competitiveness of local firms and assist the firms in expanding their markets;
4. development of informal channels of communication among local development-related organizations, by which information

regarding business and development concerns is shared more freely and effectively; and

5. ultimately, the retention and expansion of jobs, income, and investment in the community.

DEMONSTRATING A PROBUSINESS ATTITUDE

This is an almost guaranteed result of the R&E program. As soon as it is publicly announced that a local group is going to conduct the program, local businesses often start to feel more appreciated and perceive a positive shift in community attitudes toward them. This feeling is strongly reinforced by the actual visits.

In a 1984 study of Ohio R&E visitation coordinators, the demonstration of a probusiness attitude was rated as the most important goal of their respective local programs.[2] As Mary Lee Gecowets, executive director of the Urbana (Ohio) Area Chamber of Commerce said, "The R&E program is one in which you can't lose. At the very least, you'll demonstrate to firms that the community appreciates them and [you will] probably be able to help a few firms."

One of this book's authors conducted a 1987 telephone survey of local R&E coordinators in five states.[3] According to this study, an important reason often cited for expressing the community's positive attitudes toward local firms is that many communities have neglected their most important resource, existing local firms. Debra Eckes, economic research director for the Green Bay Area (Wisconsin) Chamber of Commerce, stated: "Instead of thinking in terms of 'growth,' this last deep recession has sobered us a lot. We're thinking now that we ought to at least give some thought to what our community already has."

Karen Crausby, director of the Catoosa County (Georgia) Economic Development Commission, echoed this sentiment. "We're saying, 'Look, we realize that maybe 70 percent or more of our jobs are created by existing industries. We're not forgetting that. So consider expanding here before you go outside the county.' I went to [local business leaders] and said, 'Let's go over this quiz and answer some basic questions. I want to answer your questions.' That's when they know you're really there to help. . . . So many communities can lose an existing industry because they didn't pay attention to it, to its needs; they didn't listen to its complaints. . . . Now, when we prepare a brochure or press release, we send it to our existing industries. When one of them expands, we tell it we're glad it's here. You need to treat it just like you would someone you're trying to recruit into the county."

Steven Heller, the coordinator of training for new local R&E programs for New Jersey Bell Telephone, emphasizes that the attitude of local government is very important in whether a firm decides to relocate or stay in the community. "The David Birch work[4] basically says that the attitude of local government is as important to this decision-making process as any other single thing. . . . It's *very* important."

By mobilizing volunteers from the local chamber of commerce, government, educational institutions, and other development-related agencies to express a probusiness attitude, one increases the likelihood that business owners and managers will choose to stay and expand within the community. As noted, the visits themselves are an important means of communicating this attitude. One measure of the extent to which the probusiness attitude has been conveyed successfully, therefore, is simply the number of visits made. In addition, the number of media stories about the local R&E program and the contributions of existing firms is a good proxy measure of "probusiness attitude" impact. Finally, the publication of a final program report, which demonstrates that the program is more than just a public relations event, can contribute to the probusiness attitude.

In many of the early programs, expressing a positive attitude toward business was often the only goal and primary success of the R&E efforts. Yet, if the program participants limit their sight to only this public relations goal, subsequent expansion of jobs and income is less likely to occur.

COOPERATIVE SPIRIT AMONG LOCAL DEVELOPMENT GROUPS

While few groups see developing a spirit of cooperation among local development groups as their primary goal when first launching the program, they soon come to view it as an important side benefit. A recent case study of one local Ohio R&E program suggests that cooperation occurs and is so highly valued partly because the local development leaders come to discover that they share important common interests and values.[5] From this discovery of shared intentions, and through the development of friendships among development leaders, powerful networks emerge. As one participant said, "we're all pulling in the same direction."

Local R&E coordinators in many states have attested to the considerable capacity of the program to facilitate cooperation concerning local development projects and plans, even where development leaders had once considered one another as rivals. By conducting a community-wide survey of firms to identify not only their needs and complaints but also their desires about future local development, R&E groups can formulate development plans that are founded upon widespread consensus.

Jack Marineau, director of Moscow, Idaho's Economic Development Commission, explained that prior to the R&E program his community had been sharply divided concerning local development issues. Citizens complaints and concerns is kept confidential. This benefits both the firms and the local organizations with which the firms sometimes are in conflict.

The firm, whose concerns are identified by the visitation, benefits by knowing, as Catoosa County's Karen Crausby said, "that someone cares about you," and by often having its problems resolved. Debra Eckes, of the Greater Green Bay Area Chamber of Commerce, told the story of a local firm that had lost thousands of dollars from periodic flooding of a nearby drainage ditch. The local R&E task force, comprised of local chamber, government, and other leaders, was able to resolve this problem "within two days of our finding out about it."

The organizations toward which firm complaints are being directed in the visitation interviews also benefit, by being able either to resolve a problem or to explain why the problem cannot or need not be resolved. In a few cases, as one R&E coordinator explained, "the firm's complaint proves not to be well-founded, so you can't just assume that the business is always right. But what you *do* need to do is find *out* whether they really do have a problem and then help whenever you can."

A firm in one community, for example, felt that the local utility company had been providing poor service because it had "refused" to provide a particular kind of current. The problem was relayed by the R&E task force to the utility company manager who, in turn, investigated and learned that such current would not be appropriate for the firm's equipment. As a result, the business owner thanked the utility manager for "taking the time to come out here" and for explaining the utility's actions. The utility executive, meanwhile, appreciated being able, he said, to "satisfy them that we are here, that we care, and that we want to help them *grow*." Thus, action is not necessarily required to solve some of the problems identified through the visitation process.

By keeping information regarding local business concerns confidential, businesses interviewed by the R&E volunteers as well as local development organizations are saved unnecessary embarrassment. Thus, leaders of these organizations benefit by being able to become more effective, through their comprehensive knowledge of business concerns, without having to suffer any loss in credibility.

DATA ON COMMUNITY STRENGTHS AND WEAKNESSES

The survey forms used by most states' R&E programs ask questions concerning: whether the firm is considering relocation, closure, or expansion; what specific problems or complaints the firm has; whether and in what ways the firm might wish assistance in resolving these problems; and what the businesses' perceptions are regarding the community as a place in which to do business. By collecting and aggregating this survey information, the local program is able to generate affiliated with the local university had been interested in retaining current economic assets, Marineau explained, while the business community advocated a policy of aggressive growth and firm recruitment. Business groups debated with environmental conservationist groups. Finally, those who owned and managed existing firms sometimes feared the potential competitive threats that newly attracted firms might constitute.

As a result, Marineau said, efforts to formulate and enact development plans in Moscow were often impeded. Marineau sees the R&E survey process as having been crucial in making "ours a communitywide organization. It gave us credence within all of the diverse groups in our community. . . . Right at the beginning, our committee was seen as not being a special interest group, but as a group which had the interests of the community as a whole in mind. And then, that's the group that worked to form a plan of action [after the survey process]."

While the survey process removes barriers to local cooperation, this is not the only aspect of the program that does so. The formation of an R&E task force to respond to concerns identified by the visitation survey may also play an important role. In one community, there had been such divisiveness between the leaders of various local factions that one leader suffered a stroke during a heated public debate. "This appalled me so much," said this community's R&E coordinator, "that I decided then and there to find a way to get people to work together. When I first heard about the R&E idea I thought this might be [that way]." By the end of the program, "these same people who had [once] fought each other are now working together—and actually enjoying it." (This local coordinator requested anonymity due to the sensitive nature of his story.)

While very few economic development programs are operated on a countywide basis with the collaboration of several cities and chambers of commerce, fourteen of the seventeen R&E visitation programs Ohio conducted in 1986–1987 were countywide programs. There is a much greater sense of cooperation and less fear of raiding in the R&E program than in industrial attraction programs.

In the R&E task force, members initially may recognize, in trying to resolve short-term problems indicated through the visitations, that they need to coordinate the efforts of their respective organizations. Over time, they often begin to express their enjoyment in the coordination process. By the conclusion of their task force responsibilities, many indicate that they have come to value highly not only the practical advantages of coordination, but also the personal benefits of cooperation.

CREATE FORUM FOR ADDRESSING PROBLEMS

One advantage of the R&E program, unlike many conventional approaches to local development, is that program participants create a nonpublic forum in which often sensitive information regarding business a wealth of information regarding the positives and negatives of the community's business climate.

The positive findings may be used by the task force member organizations and other local development groups to attract new firms to the community. Negative findings are either quietly addressed or are identified as reasons to develop new local program and policy initiatives. Negative information is essential to identify ways to improve the local business climate.

Bill Grunkemeyer explains that as a result of the Fayette County, Ohio R&E visitation survey, the R&E report found good labor/management relations among its local firms. Using these data, Grunkemeyer has been able to correct the traditional but misleading view that the county had poor labor/management relations. As a result, what had once been a major obstacle for recruiting became a centerpiece for their current attraction efforts.

UNDERSTANDING OF THE COMMUNITY'S ECONOMIC OUTLOOK

Changes in the demand for locally produced goods and services are the major determinants of the economic outlook for individual firms and, in the aggregate, for the community. Changes in the cost of production, new technology, new products, and other supply factors can influence price and, thus, the market share for a particular firm's products. While communities can seldom control these factors, they can take advantage of positive trends and minimize the costs of negative ones.

In Fayette County, Ohio, the R&E task force recommended a greater emphasis on the retail and wholesale trade sectors after examining the employment trends in these sectors, using shift-share analysis. Their examination showed that retail and wholesale trade in the county should have grown by 670 jobs from 1977 to 1985, while it actually lost 248 jobs, resulting in 918 fewer jobs than would have been expected based on national trends. The service sector had 288 fewer jobs than expected according to the shift-share analysis. Bill Grunkemeyer, the Ohio Cooperative Extension Service agent running the Fayette County economic development program, reported: "These data confirmed our need to work directly with the retail and service sectors as sources of employment rather than to just assume that spin-off jobs would be created as we had expansion in manufacturing firms. The two go hand-in-hand. The more retail and services the community has to offer the more attractive it will be to industrial firms and vice versa."

In the Greater Green Bay Area Chamber of Commerce's R&E program, according to Debra Eckes, data regarding the economic outlook for the area and individual firms has been used to: (1) identify local suppliers who can cost-competitively meet the resource needs of other local firms; (2) determine the kinds of firms which the community needs to attract to meet substantial local resource needs; (3) encourage "reverse investment" by Japanese companies in local food processing ventures; (4) establish a foreign trade zone; and (5) create a local venture capital group to assist in both new firm creation and existing small firm expansion. In other words, the Green Bay program's experience suggests the many uses of data regarding firm and community economic outlook. One important benefit of basing development plans on such data, moreover, is that plans to expand existing firms or to recruit new firms are made in ways compatible with the interests of local firms.

LOCAL ECONOMIC STRATEGIC PLANNING

Strategic planning requires a careful review of the local environment, the development of alternative strategies, and the evaluation and selection of the strategy most appropriate to local resources and preferences. Using the data collected in the business visits, the R&E task force develops and assesses ideas for local action. Some of the ideas they generate, of course, concern very specific actions or short-term projects. Other task force recommendations, however, are made with regard to longer term strategies.

For example, in Champaign County, Ohio, the R&E task force recommended that a permanent economic development council be established and that a half-time professional be hired to staff the council. According to Roland Patzer, Champaign County R&E coordinator, the achievement of this strategic recommendation came much faster than expected and wouldn't have been possible without the R&E planning process.

However, the visitation survey process not only generates new ideas for local development projects and strategies, but it also may be used to collect data useful for legitimizing pre-existing demands for new or increased support from state and federal governments. Survey information regarding the transportation concerns of local firms, for example, was acquired by the Logan County, Ohio, program. "We've known all along about the need to widen the highway in the county," said Lee Dorsey, the executive director of the county's Chamber of Commerce. "We've been after the state for *years* to *do* something about it. But with this *survey* data, we've got some ammunition. . . . The state keeps telling us we have to show how [widening the highway] will spur development—well, this survey shows how many businesses *need* that road widened."

PROGRAMS TO IMPROVE THE COMPETITIVENESS
OF LOCAL FIRMS

Any program that allows a firm to cut its costs of doing business puts the firm in a more competitive position in the national and international market. State programs that provide assistance with labor training, labor/management relations, marketing, management, and other information all may contribute to the firm's competitive position. Financing subsidies and tax exemptions, on the other hand, also provide a competitive edge to firms, but do not help them develop the human capital and technological expertise needed to realize permanent gains in competitiveness.

In one county, specific survey information was used to create a new program, using public sector resources to prevent a firm relocation. A firm in Washington County, Ohio, needed to add forty jobs to its work force, but had to reject nearly 800 applicants because they could not pass the firm's mathematics test. Emerson Shimp, the R&E coordinator, developed a response team that met with administrators from the chemical plants and educational administrators in the region. As a result, a chemical workers training program was developed to meet the needs of local employers. This program enabled local chemical firms to hire local people rather than recruiting employees from outside the area.

Howard Wise, manager of the Office of Industrial Development at the Ohio Department of Development, one of the cosponsors of the Ohio R&E program, points out that personal contact is often essential in helping firms use the best state and federal programs. "The volunteer R&E visitation teams give our state staff a tremendous multiplier effect. This allows my staff to focus its attention on the most critical R&E problems where the state can get the greatest bang for the buck. There is no question that communities with R&E programs can tap into state programs better than those without."

Sometimes programs already exist to support firm retention and expansion. However, survey information may enable local leaders to ensure that these resources are directed to better meet the level of local need for them. Tim Ashmore, industrial relations director for the Columbus (Georgia) Chamber of Commerce, describes how the chamber has for some years operated a variety of committees concerning such matters as employer-employee relations, management training, marketing workshops, and the like. What the visitation process allowed the chamber to do, he explained, was refer information regarding a firm's need for various kinds of services to the relevant committees. Chamber members, who volunteer to serve on these committees, would then contact the firm and explain the nature and values of the services available.

Thus, those benefiting include not only the firms demanding the services but also the organizations whose goal it is to market and deliver such services. Chambers of commerce, state agencies, local community colleges, and a wide variety of other service providers benefit by an increase in demand for, use of, and appreciation of their services. One state department of development official confidentially remarked that local R&E programs "greatly improve our effectiveness . . . because they make people more *aware* of what we're able to offer them."

DEVELOPING INFORMAL COMMUNICATION NETWORKS

As suggested earlier, local R&E task forces bring together leaders from a variety of local development-related organizations. As they come to recognize more fully their shared interests and goals, it appears that greater mutual respect and friendship also may develop. Observation of one task force's interaction indicates that new channels of communication develop.

Prior to the R&E program, representatives of many local development-related organizations interact through more formal channels, via such means as public statements, written memoranda, and sometimes litigation. Membership in the task force, however, appears to make it more difficult for those who have interacted only in formal ways to continue to do so.

Having served together on the local task force, Karen Crausby of Catoosa County's Economic Development Commission explained, "Now I can call him up and say, 'I've found out about this problem here. Can you see what you can do about it?" Such networking enables local firms to resolve their problems more quickly and effectively.

Most communities, of course, have such networks. One problem is that in many localities the networks are limited to a fairly restricted membership and often do not include leaders from the wide range of development-related organizations that businesses need to draw upon to meet their diverse needs. Through the R&E program, these networks are widened.

RETENTION AND EXPANSION OF JOBS, INCOME, AND INVESTMENT

Generally, economic development researchers will argue that one can prove anything with a few well selected examples. They would claim that you need to examine growth rates and other impacts of an R&E program in communities with and without R&E visitation programs.

Only pilot efforts have been completed in such comparative research, suggesting very high benefit cost ratios.[6] Much more research is needed. As the number of communities using the R&E program increases, the feasibility of this comparative approach improves. Directors of state R&E training programs in several states have remarked about the frequent program design changes they have made, based on improvements suggested by local participants and their experiences. Action-oriented professionals should encourage such comparative research as a means of better demonstrating the success of their R&E programs.

Further qualitative research also is needed. Such research, which more open-endedly asks participants to describe and explain the advantages and disadvantages of R&E as a local development strategy, may provide rich information with which to note the variety of tangible and intangible costs and benefits of the program.

While the authors have had to rely heavily on Ohio examples due to budget constraints in contacting other states, it appears that a number of other states are starting R&E visitation programs. While the visitation programs are only a small part of the total R&E program, they are a good place to start. The programs not only help local groups set priorities that meet the needs of existing firms and improve the desirability of the community to new firms, but also build the capacity of local groups to implement economic development. The growing number of states implementing such programs strongly suggests the increasing importance of this approach to local development.

NOTES

1. This chapter is reprinted with permission from a bulletin written by the authors for the North Central Regional Center for Rural Development, Iowa State University.

2. George W. Morse, Kathryn Wilson, and Steven I. Gordon, "Local Industry Visitation Programs: Policy Research and Recommendations," report prepared for the Ohio Labor Management Committee and the Urban Affairs Program, Ohio State University (Columbus, Oh.: Ohio State University, Department of Agricultural Economics and Rural Sociology, Mar. 1985), 20–22.

3. Interviews completed by Robert McLaughlin in collaboration with George Morse.

4. David L. Birch, *The Job Generation Process* (Cambridge, Mass.: MIT Program on Neighborhood and Regional Change, 1979).

5. Robert T. McLaughlin, "Making Connections in the Heartland: An Educator's Case Study of a Local Business Retention and Expansion Program," Ph.D. diss., Ohio State University, 1987.

6. Morse, Wilson, and Gordon, 1985.

REFERENCES

Birch, David L. "The Job Generation Process." Prepared for MIT Program on Neighborhood and Regional Change, MIT, Cambridge, Mass., 1979, photocopy.
McLaughlin, Robert T. "Making Connections in the Heartland: An Educator's Case Study of a Local Business Retention and Expansion Program." Ph.D. diss, Ohio State University, 1987.

⑨

Impacts of the Washington County R&E Program

GEORGE MORSE

Washington County, Ohio, was the first county to participate in the new Ohio Business Retention and Expansion Program, which started in February 1986. This countywide program was coordinated by Emerson Shimp, Economic Development Extension agent, with George Morse, Ohio State University Extension economist, who provided the training programs. Since the approach used is nearly identical to that described in Chapter 4, this chapter describes Washington County, the organizational features unique to the Washington County program, and its major accomplishments to date.

BACKGROUND DATA, WASHINGTON COUNTY, OHIO

Washington County, Ohio, sits on the Ohio River about 120 miles from Columbus, the state capital. The county's 1984 population was 64,799, reflecting growth of 13.4 percent since 1970, nearly all of which occurred before 1980. Marietta, the county seat, had a 1984 population of 16,535; Belpre, a part of the Parkersburg, West Virginia, Standard Metropolitan Statistical Area (SMSA), had a 1984 population of 7,049; the rest of the county's 1984 population was 41,215. Both cities lost population slightly while economic growth occurred in the rest of the county.

The private sector labor force was 30,172 in 1985, up by 14 percent from 1977. The unemployment rate in 1985 was 11.7 percent or 3,548 individuals without work.

The major losses in employment in Washington County from 1977 to 1985 occurred in three sectors: manufacturing, losing 943 jobs; construction, losing 278 jobs; and transportation, losing 103 jobs. In all three industries these declines were primarily due to losses in local employment that exceeded those expected from national trends (See Table 9.1).

TABLE 9.1. Shift-Share Analysis, Washington County, 1977–1985

Sector	Actual Changes in Jobs	Expected Changes in Jobs	Differences in Actual & Expected Changes
Mining	550	29	521
Construction	−278	372	−650
Manufacturing	−943	− 69	−874
Transportation	−103	246	−349
Finance	92	177	− 85
Retail Trade	792	882	− 90
Wholesale	490	164	326
Services	837	1556	−719
TOTAL	1437	3357	−1920

In Washington County, manufacturing firms are generally in industries with declining employment in the United States. Based on the national rates of decline in these industries, the county's manufacturing sector should have lost 69 jobs. But the county actually lost 943 manufacturing jobs, or 874 more than expected (See Table 9.2).

Nine of the ten major manufacturing industries in Washington County are in declining sectors (Table 9.2). More importantly, local losses in eight of the ten manufacturing sectors exceeded national trends. For example, the fabricated metals industry lost 348 more jobs than would have been expected from national trends, which is about one third of the total local loss. These data alone do not provide sufficient information to judge whether the fabricated metals industry is losing its comparative advantage and sales to other firms or whether it has adopted labor-saving technology that improves its comparative advantage. But the data do point out the source of the declines.

TABLE 9.2. Shift-Share Analysis of Manufacturing Employment, Washington County, 1977–1985

Sector	Actual Changes in Jobs	Expected Changes in Jobs	Differences in Actual & Expected Changes
Food & kindred products	− 97	− 16	− 80
Lumber & wood products	− 39	23	− 62
Printing & publishing	0	58	− 58
Chemical & allied	199	− 13	211
Rubber & plastics	− 59	109	−168
Stone, clay, & glass	− 44	− 19	− 24
Primary metal ind.	−209	−512	303
Fabricated metals	−335	13	−348
Machinery, ex elect	− 42	− 1	− 42
Excluded sectors	−318	236	−606
TOTAL	−943	− 70	−874

REASONS FOR STARTING THE R&E PROGRAM

During the early 1980s, the Washington County commissioners started to explore the potential for developing an economic development office and hiring a professional to conduct local programs. After considerable study of the options available, they approached Emerson Shimp, Community Development Extension agent in Washington County about working full-time in this area. The county agreed to provide funding to the Ohio Cooperative Extension Service so that a program assistant could be hired to carry on Emerson's work in 4-H and community development.

The Washington County Extension Service formally became involved in economic development in February 1986, when Shimp became the full-time economic development county agent. Shimp had been a 4-H and community development extension agent in Washington County for sixteen years prior to this change. Shimp's academic background is in agricultural education and farm management, rather than in fields normally associated with economic development. Yet, he had more than sixteen years of experience in working with volunteer groups and in problem-solving in a community setting.

Why did Shimp decide to invest considerable time in the R&E visitation program during the critical first year in his new economic development program? Why not emphasize the attraction of branch plants, the creation of new firms, or the reduction of consumer leakages rather than focus on the existing firms? First, Shimp points out that he and other local leaders needed to understand the existing industrial base and the concerns of these firms as a basis for planning long-term efforts.

Frequently, new development professionals are forced to undertake major projects before they become familiar with the local leadership and the local concerns. The R&E visitation program quickly gave Shimp a familiarity with local leaders and issues while also giving him time to understand these. Second, he needed a program with both a quick and certain payoff and one that gave high visibility to the new economic development effort. While the R&E program appeared almost certain to achieve the public relations goal as well as offering the opportunity to work on more tangible problems, Shimp knew the odds of attracting new businesses were slim. Through the program, the new economic development office received media coverage on nearly a weekly basis, with major articles and special features appearing at the kickoff of the project and at the final meeting.

Third, the R&E visitation program provided a means to involve a wide range of groups and communities in an action-oriented effort. In contrast, both attraction and entrepreneurship strategies usually result in only a few winners, possibly making those left out feel that the program had discriminated against them. Fourth, the applied research results from the firm survey and from published data provided an opportunity for the community leadership to understand both the strengths and weaknesses of the community with respect to economic development. Shimp expected this improved understanding to result in more carefully developed economic development plans.

After the program was completed, Shimp's only regret was that he served primarily as a coordinator, going on only a handful of the firm visits himself. While time probably would not have permitted him to go on all ninety-nine visits, he suggests that other development professionals consider going on as many as possible.

ORGANIZING FOR THE R&E PROGRAM

Economic Development Practitioners Group

Recognizing the need for a team effort and the current fragmentation in local development efforts, Shimp convened an "Economic Development Practitioners Group" as the first step in his economic development program. All those who would define themselves as economic development practitioners were invited to participate in this group. The initial objective was to simply exchange information on programs and build rapport among the individual practitioners. The group included the staff from the local chambers of commerce, regional planning specialists, labor training program representatives, bureau of employment services staff members, utility economic development professionals, agents from the Ohio Technology Transfer Organization, and others.

At each meeting of the "Economic Development Practitioners Group," everyone was given an opportunity for a three-minute update. Then one group presented a twenty-minute description of its program. Over time, the individuals in this group developed the empathy and rapport necessary to work as a local development team. These meetings also provided Shimp an opportunity to become acquainted with the local development resources, making the process of referral of firms to the best source of help much more effective.

As a spin-off of this group, the labor-related programs held an informal meeting to discuss three common problems. First, they did not have sufficient time to keep firms fully aware of their services and to provide detailed assistance to firms actually needing help. Second, when they made calls to firms to explain their services, they sometimes received a cold reception because another labor-related program had just spent thirty to forty minutes with the firm manager. Third, many firms saw the labor programs as redundant and were confused about the different services each offers.

To solve these problems, the group established "LaborNet," an informal network of all the local labor-related programs. Now, each firm is assigned to one member of LaborNet who explains all of the labor programs and maintains primary contact with the firm. This not only builds trust between the firm and the LaborNet representative but also saves the firm manager time and allows the LaborNet representative a chance to better understand the firm's needs.

Advisory Committees and R&E Task Force

In Washington County, the structure of the R&E program was slightly different than that described in Chapter 4. An overall advisory committee provided the general directions for the Extension Service program, while three separate R&E task forces were established to handle issues or problems in each of the areas covered by the county's chambers of commerce: Marietta, Belpre, and Waterford/Beverly. Since the role of the task force is to handle local government problems, Washington County leaders felt there should be as direct communications as possible between the firms and those responsible for resolving the problems. Further, there was some reluctance to have local problems aired in other parts of the county. The advisory committee, rather than the individual task forces, developed the final recommendations for the R&E program.

Practice Visits

Three practice visits were conducted in March 1986, but unlike the description in Chapter 4, no meeting was held with the R&E task force.

Since three visits were scheduled for one day, there was not time for a task force meeting.

Training for Volunteers

Three separate, identical training sessions were held in early April 1986, one in each of the three communities. The sessions were scheduled at three separate times to give volunteers as many opportunities as possible to participate. Interestingly, all of the volunteers at the Belpre meeting were from other locations, suggesting that volunteers were more interested in the time of the meeting than the location. Each meeting followed the format described in Chapter 4, with about twenty to twenty-five minutes allocated for the loudspeaker telephone discussion with the coordinator of the Mercer County R&E program. In total, more than fifty local leaders participated in the three training sessions.

Each of the visitors was given a card to indicate their first, second, and third choices for teammates. Still, the coordinator reserved the right to match the leaders as best he could and then mailed out the team assignments. Because of the large number of visits and volunteers, the teams were separated into several groups. The visits made by each group were staggered so that Shimp was not overwhelmed with follow-up work.

The volunteers completed their visits over four and one half months, ending in August. Three changes might be made if this was repeated. First, the volunteers would have been assigned prior to the training and given packets allowing them to make their visits immediately. Second, all volunteers would be encouraged to call their firms immediately. To handle the large volume of follow-up, a team of volunteer consultants would have been used.

Developing the Recommendations

Only one two-hour meeting was scheduled to review the data and to select the recommendations from those provided by the Ohio State University. It became evident that this was insufficient, so the meeting was extended to three and one half hours, with a small group working on the final recommendations.

Final Community Meeting

An invitation-only meeting on the final results, held September 29, 1986, attracted 165 county, regional, and state economic development leaders. The evening meeting was held at the Lafayette Hotel, a richly refurbished hotel on the Ohio River. Following wine and hors d'oeuvres, Shimp introduced many notables in the audience. George Morse presented highlights from the survey, and Shimp then summarized the recommendations. The meeting had an air of celebration rather than one of debate and discussion. Participants were encouraged to examine the findings and recommendations and to invite the R&E coordinator or task force to speak to their group.

ACCOMPLISHMENTS OF WASHINGTON COUNTY'S R&E PROGRAM

The R&E task force made eleven specific recommendations, ranging from continuing the R&E program to providing additional information on state and local taxes. (See Appendix 9.1 for the full set of recommendations). These following accomplishments have been achieved during the ten-month period from October 1986 to August 1987.

Continuation of the Business R&E Program

The survey of the ninety-eight local firms produced a number of results that suggested the R&E program should continue on an annual basis. Twenty-three firms (53 percent) indicated that they needed assistance from local government on services. Since it was expected that firms will have similar problems on an annual basis and that the major source of employment growth would be from existing firms, the advisory committee recommended that the R&E programs be continued.

The recommendation to continue the visitation program with a focus on the service industry is being implemented. Currently the local leaders are visiting one hundred retail and service sector firms. Arrangements have been made for Dr. William Gillis of Pennsylvania State University to analyze the results. The training of the volunteers was done entirely by the local leaders based on their experience in the 1986 program.

Twenty-three follow-up visits have been made to businesses having ongoing concerns. For example, on one visit a firm in the chemical industry reported that it had to reject 800 applicants for forty jobs because they lacked basic math skills. After several follow-up meetings, a special Chemical Workers Training Program was set up at the Washington Technical College and Washington County Career Center with funding from the Joint Training and Partnership Act. To date, fifty local individuals have been trained by the program and are employed in related positions. A new two-year chemical operators program is being offered by Washington Technical College this fall.

While there was some interest in repeating the visits to all manufacturing firms, it appeared more practical to use a mail and telephone survey to contact these firms. A mail survey was planned for October 1988.

The Retention and Expansion Advisory Committee has met once since the original survey to focus on the follow-up contacts.

Up-to-Date Information for Local Businesses

During the firm visits, the 98 firms identified 198 programs about which they would like additional information. To implement the recommendation that up-to-date information should be provided to local firms, a newsletter titled "Washington County Business Update" has been sent to 450 local firms. Seven issues have been disseminated, covering topics such as upcoming events, new regulations, exporting/importing information, taxes, and business information. This has proven to be a very effective and efficient means of sharing information on state regulations, state and local taxes, exporting, and other topics. It also keeps industries aware of the Economic Development Office.

Develop Management and Marketing Assistance

The survey of local firms found that 36 percent and 32 percent wanted additional information on marketing strategies and management, respectively. The Washington County Advisory Committee recommended that "Local resources need to coordinate efforts and explore new methods to provide assistance in management and marketing strategies."

The original survey of firms, although requiring an hour to complete, did not provide enough information on either marketing or management to develop a follow-up program. Ten organizations working on management and marketing education (Washington Technical College, Parkersburg Community College, Ohio University, Washington Community Career Center, Marietta College, American Marketing Association, Gianfornia & Associates, Offenberger & White, Marietta Chamber of Commerce) met to work on this issue. They developed a survey of two hundred businesses in both Washington County and Wood County, West Virginia, to collect more specific information on the needs for marketing and management information. The mail survey had an excellent response rate (54 percent).

The top three management or marketing topics that chief executive officers identified as areas in which they need the most assistance were: decision making with emphasis on planning, motivating and evaluating personnel, and finances, with emphasis on cash flow. The organizations are incorporating the survey results in their 1987–1988 programs.

Design an Import Substitution Effort

The R&E visitation survey of local firms found fifty-two products currently being purchased outside the county that firms felt might be economically produced in the county. One way to encourage greater local purchasing of Washington County products is to ensure that firms are aware of each others' products and services. Trade shows are one means of achieving this goal.

A local trade show, Expo '87, was held April 2 and 3 in the Marietta College Field House. The Expo featured sixty-three booths by local firms and six booths by local organizations. Invitations to a special private showing were sent to businesses within a 75-mile radius and to preferred customers of exhibitors. One hundred twenty-five businesses attended this private showing on the first day. The public show attracted approximately 300 people including high school student groups.

Exhibitors indicated they did identify business leads and would participate in another local trade show if held again next year. The cost to companies to exhibit in Expo '87 and to entertain their clients was cited as much less than exhibiting in large trade shows. Methods to increase attendance by potential buyers was identified as an area to emphasize the next year.

EVALUATION OF THE WASHINGTON COUNTY R&E PROGRAM

What is the bottom line? Did the R&E program in Washington retain or expand any jobs? Did any firms that might have closed or moved out of town stay in the community as a result of the R&E program? Did any firms expand as a result of the R&E program? How many of the fifty jobs retained in the county as a result of the new labor training program for the chemical plant should be credited to the R&E program that identified the issue, and how many to the technical school that provided the training? Clearly, these are difficult but important research issues that need further investigation on both a conceptual and empirical level. But even without this in-depth research it appears that the Washington County R&E visitation program has been highly successful. Five pieces of evidence lead to this conclusion.

The first evidence of the success of the R&E visitation program is that the three chambers of commerce decided to repeat the process with retail and service sector firms. This second set of visits to one hundred firms started in May 1987 and is now 70 percent complete.

The second means of measuring success is to look at the number of recommendations from the final report that have been achieved. On this score, Washington County is doing exceptionally well, having some results on every one of the activities recommended by the R&E task force.

The third indication of success is that the county commissioners continued the funding of the new economic development office, which had as its major project the R&E program. As one of the commissioners said when speaking about the R&E program and Shimp's position: "This was the best $50,000 we've spent in the county!"

A fourth clue on the success of this program has been interest of other counties in duplicating the program and establishing a full-time county extension agent in economic development. Shimp's presentations on the Washington County experience at two state conferences have encouraged twenty-two other counties to start new R&E programs.

The fifth, and most convincing, evidence that the R&E program has had positive results is that Emerson Shimp recommends that all new county extension agents start with this economic development strategy.

While none of these clues is hard evidence that the R&E program has retained or expanded jobs, they are very encouraging. Although additional research is needed to document the changes created by the R&E visitation program and follow-up efforts, Washington County leaders are convinced that they need to continue helping their existing businesses and are proud of the achievements of their R&E program.

APPENDIX 9.1

SUMMARY of the 1986

WASHINGTON COUNTY
BUSINESS RETENTION AND EXPANSION VISITATION
PROGRAM REPORT

This summary provides highlights of the Retention and Expansion Report. Consult the 1986 Washington County Retention and Expansion Report for details. Copies are available in the Washington County Extension Office - Economic Development, County Commissioner's Office, Mayor's Office, Chambers of Commerce and most libraries and offices serving local businesses.

Sponsored by:

Belpre Chamber of Commerce
Beverly-Waterford Chamber of Commerce
Marietta Area Chamber of Commerce

Technical Assistance Provided by:

Ohio Cooperative Extension Service
The Ohio State University

The Ohio Department of Development

BACKGROUND ON R & E BUSINESS VISITATION PROGRAM

The Retention and Expansion Business
Visitation Program in Washington County
involved 53 volunteers visiting 98 local
manufacturing and non-manufacturing firms.
The survey represented 83 percent of the
targeted industry employment and 41 percent
of the total employment in the county.
Each firm responded to 23 questions during
the Firm visit. This data is the basis for
this report.

The visitation program also responded to
immediate requests and concerns of local
firms. Local officials and economic
development practitioners were excellent in
responding to these requests.

Some of those assisting included:

American Marketing Association

Belpre Chamber of Commerce

Beverly-Waterford Chamber of Commerce

Buckeye Hills-Hocking Valley Regional
Development District

Marietta Area Chamber of Commerce

Marietta College Business Resource Center

Marietta SCORE-ACE Chapter

Mayors of Belpre, Beverly and Marietta

Ohio Bureau of Employment Service

Ohio Industrial Training Program

Ohio Technology Transfer Organization

Washington County Career Center

Washington County Commissioners

Washington County Community Improvement
Corporation

Washington Technical College

Washington-Monroe County Community Action
Organization

Withrow Linked Deposit Program

Selected Business Leaders

An employment shift-share analysis was
completed by George Morse, Extension
Economist, Ohio Cooperative Extension
Service, The Ohio State University. This
analysis examined the employment trends in
Washington County from 1977 to late 1984 and
compared these trends to Ohio and national
trends. The employment trends analysis and
the local data from the visitation program
provided the backdrop for the Washington
County Retention and Expansion Advisory
Committee recommendations.

SURVEY'S MAJOR FINDINGS

Employment Changes
Overall private sector employment grew by
14.0 percent in Washington County from 1977
to late 1984. This was much better then
Ohio's average growth rate (9.6%) but much
lower than the U.S. rate (25.3%). A
decline occurred in employment in the
manufacturing sector but manufacturing
still employs 28 percent of the county work
force. Retail trade and Services
experienced increases to 24 percent and 18
percent of employment, respectively. The
decline in manufacturing employment
occurred in every sector except chemicals
and allied products.

Market Location
For the 56 manufacturing firms in the
survey, an average of 26 percent of their
sales were in the county, 19 percent in
Ohio and 53 percent in the United States.
Only three percent of the sales were
exported.

Markets and Customers
More than 85 percent of all raw materials
and supplies were purchased outside the
county. While most will continue, local
firms identified 52 possibilities for local
production.

Expansion and Moving Plans
Most firms (72%) have no plans to move
and have room to expand. Thirty-eight
percent reported plans to expand their
plant.

Information Requested
The most frequently requested information was on Marketing Strategies, Management Seminars and New State Regulations. Exporting Information was requested by 15 percent of the firms although only 3 percent of their current sales are exported. Financing Programs were requested by 29 percent, Labor Training by 19 percent, and Relations by 15 percent of the firms.

Governmental Concerns and Assistance
Twenty-three firms indicated they needed assistance from local government on services, i.e., water, sewer, police, zoning, etc. Water and sewer were the most frequently cited local concerns.

State Government complaints were voiced by 41 percent of the firms. The concerns most frequently cited included: Workers compensation (23.3% of complaints), taxes (16.6%) and slow processing of permits (10%).

Business Climate and Location Factors
The survey asked firms to rate 12 location factors for their business. These included cost factors, i.e., labor, taxes, transportation, energy, occupancy, as well as non-economic factors, i.e., labor attitude, availability, utility dependability, schools and quality of life. As a place to do business, 93 percent of the firms surveyed rated Washington County as excellent (19%) or good (74%). The best feature of the community most commonly cited was community attitude.

RECOMMENDATIONS FOR BUSINESS RETENTION AND EXPANSION IN WASHINGTON COUNTY

The Washington County Retention and Expansion Advisory Committee reviewed the survey results and shift-share employment analysis and makes the following recommendations:

I.   Continue Business Retention and Expansion Programs.

The major source of employment growth in Washington County is likely to be the businesses already there.

Three directions were recommended for future R & E efforts, including:

A. Continue the visitation programs with focus on the service industry.

B. Make Follow-up Visits to 1986 participants with on-going concerns or informational needs.

C. Continue the Retention and Expansion Advisory Committee.

II.   Provide Up-To-Date Information to Local Businesses.

Washington County's business resources are broader than similar communities and of higher quality. These resources need to be coordinated to meet the needs of local business. The smaller business has limited time and resources requiring creative methods to provide access to information and assistance. The teleconferencing program should be continued as a means of linking businessmen and experts at low cost.

III.   Developed Management and Marketing Assistance.

Local resources need to coordinate efforts and explore new methods to provide assistance in management and marketing strategies.

IV.   Provide Information on New State Regulations.

A local system for securing and distributing information needs to be developed. As a first step, the Small Business Register is being obtained for local distribution.

V.   Establish Labor Management programs.

Although labor management attitudes and relations were perceived by the majority as good to be excellent, there were significant numbers of firms noting it less than good. An ad hoc committee needs to explore possibilities for improvement.

VI.   Name an Export Marketing Committee.
Local support and assistance needs to

focus on the firms indicating an interest in exporting.

VII. Design an Import Substitution Effort.

Developing local sources for goods and services purchased by businesses offers potential for expansion. A committee needs to focus efforts at development of local sources of purchased imports. The feasibility of the 52 products suggested by firms needs to be expressed.

VIII. Disseminate Information About State and Local Taxes.

Taxes are a major concern of business. However, detailed data on taxes in Ohio and Washington County relative to other areas is not readily available. Information about tax structure and comparisons to other communities needs to be provided to businesses.

Prepared by:

Emerson Shimp, County Agent,
  Economic Development, OCES

George Morse, Specialist,
  Agricultrural Economics, OCES

9/86 - 500

Issued in furtherance of Cooperative Extension work, Acts of May 8 and June 30, 1914, in cooperation with the U.S. Department of Agriculture, J. Michael Sprott, Director of the Ohio Cooperative Extension Service, The Ohio State University.

10

Success in a Small Rural County: The Champaign County Experience

ELLEN HAGEY

Champaign County was one of the first communities to implement the current Business Retention and Expansion (R&E) Program in Ohio. Although similar to the theoretical model of the R&E program, which has been explained earlier, Champaign County's program, like all programs, deviated slightly from the general concept. Despite the minor variations in this program, the outcomes resemble those presented in Figure 1.1. That is, the program demonstrated the community's pro-business attitude, helped to develop local leadership, and enabled local leaders to collect data about the community and its firms.

Champaign County is a rural area about forty-five miles west of Columbus and northeast of Dayton. Urbana is the principal city and site of industrial concentration. Based on 1984 data, nearly half of the county's labor force works in manufacturing. Manufacturing establishments, however, represent only about 10 percent of all establishments. Unemployment has been relatively low in the county, only 8.1 percent in 1985 and 1986.

THE REASON FOR IMPLEMENTING AN R&E PROGRAM

In 1985, several local leaders in Champaign County began meeting as a group to address local economic issues, specifically job creation, industrial composition, supply of labor, concentration of employment, and county development. These local leaders represented, among other organizations interested in economic development, the chamber of commerce, utilities, job placement services, labor training programs, and local businesses. The group decided that it needed to gather information about its existing businesses to evaluate more accurately the local economy. Mary Lee Gecowets, from the county's Chamber of Commerce, suggested the Ohio R&E program as a potential initiative to gather such information. Gencowets had learned of the program during a week-long economic seminar at the Ohio State University (OSU) during the spring of 1983.

For some communities, interest in the R&E program has stemmed from adverse economic circumstances, such as a large employer announcing plans to close or relocate, or the continuing outmigration of the labor force, or the persistence of high unemployment. In Champaign County, however, the adoption of the R&E program stemmed more from general interest in improving the area's economy than from recent economic crises. In 1986 unemployment was relatively low and no plants had closed or announced relocation plans. The local leaders wanted to implement an R&E program because they saw it as the first step to economic development, not as a reaction to negative economic conditions.

IMPLEMENTING THE PROGRAM

Since the program is sponsored in part by the Ohio Cooperative Extension Service (OCES), Jack Sommers, the local extension agent and member of this initial group of concerned citizens, obtained a slide set about the program. Afterward, a group of four local leaders including Jack Sommers, Mary Lee Gecowets, and Roland Patzer traveled to OSU to meet with George Morse, state specialist for the Extension Service and developer of the R&E program. Based on this meeting, the local leaders decided to implement the program. Currently, because the demand is high and the resources limited, communities must apply for participation in Ohio's program.

The program had changed significantly since the time Mary Lee Gecowets had first heard of it in 1983. At that time, the R&E program consisted only of the slide set that communities viewed. Based on that information, communities simply implemented their own programs.[1]

In 1986, the program had evolved dramatically. The slide set was still distributed, but OSU and OCES played a much larger role in the implementation of the program. George Morse had developed the program into a structured, six-month project that involved specified steps including mandatory practice visits, training, educational materials, data analysis, final reports, and community meetings. This structured approach was intended to increase the likelihood of stimulating long-term economic development as a result of the program. Many communities in Ohio have some sort of R&E program but most end when the visitations end. By involving key local leaders as coordinators, volunteers and task force members, and most important, by analyzing the data collected and writing recommendations based on that analysis, the potential for the program to foster long-term economic development increases.

In the early spring of 1986, a steering committee (task force) was formed for the program. The committee consisted of twelve local leaders from both public and private sectors:

Chairman, Private Industry Council
   Roland Patzer
Executive Director, Urbana Area Chamber of Commerce
   Mary Lee Gecowets
County Extension Agent, Ohio Cooperative Extension Service
   Jack Sommers
County Commissioner
   Grover Foulk
Mayor, City of Urbana
   Lewis Moore
Superintendent of Urbana Public Schools
   Ralph Nix
Owner, Sweeting Tire, Inc.
   Charles Sweeting
Professor Emeritus, Wilburforce University
   Arthur Stokes
Owner, Guild Galleries
   Phil Kern
President, Citizens National Bank
   Marvin Humphrey
Director of Development, City of Urbana
   Patricia King
Economic Development Consultant, Columbia Gas of Ohio
   Paul Clapsaddle

The steering committee's role in the program was threefold: to nominate volunteers and assign them to firms; to address concerns or problems cited by firms; and to write the recommendations for the final report based on the findings from the visits. Although the members of the steering committee had never worked as a group previously, most had worked together in smaller groups and were somewhat familiar with each other's resources. According to Mary Lee Gecowets, even with this familiarity, the members had to get used to each other: "When you set a different goal, the dynamics of the group change. Still, they were committed from day one."

Roland Patzer, who was one of the members of the initial group of local leaders and who ran the local Joint Training Partnership Act (a state-funded labor training program), acted as the coordinator for the program. As the retired president of Urbana College and the president-elect of the Urbana Area Rotary Club, Patzer brought to the coordinator's position a unique set of leadership experiences that helped unite the local leaders in the public and private sectors. As a result, the superintendent of schools and a professor emeritus were members of the steering committee.

Champaign County's business visits began in April 1986 when the local leaders conducted practice visits with two local industries. Later that week, thirty-eight volunteer visitors attended a two-and-one-half hour training session designed to explain the purpose and structure of the program and the volunteers' critical role in its success.

The Champaign County steering committee placed considerable attention on recruiting volunteers. As Jack Sommers explained: "Selecting the proper volunteers and the people who could do the best job was certainly an important facet of the R&E program and one of the things that we tried to do is select the people who were busy, involved, and respected by various businesses in the community."

According to Mary Lee Gecowets, volunteer recruitment was not difficult because local interest in the program already existed. Although some of the volunteers had questions about the program and some reservations about conducting an hour-long interview with the president of a local industry, they became much more confident after the training.

During the training each volunteer received a "visitor packet" that included information about the R&E program, suggestions for conducting an effective visit, surveys, and industrial outlook summaries about the industries they were assigned to visit. Volunteers were strongly encouraged to read their summaries so they knew or were at least aware of the economic status of the industry they were visiting and the extent to which certain factors, such as foreign competition, were affecting that particular industry.

Also included in the packet were the volunteer's team assignment and firm assignment. Volunteers visited firms in teams of two to not only demonstrate the community's interest in its industry but also to facilitate the actual interview. With two visitors, one asked the questions, the other recorded the answers. To enable the volunteers to contact their industries immediately, the name of the industry, the name of the contact person, the industry's telephone number, and its address were printed on each survey.

The volunteers visited fifty-four industries and businesses of the original seventy-two targeted in about two months. Only four of the eighteen industries and businesses not visited refused to participate in the program. These firms were branches of large retail companies. The other fourteen firms were not visited because of time constraints and prior commitments. The fifty-four firms visited employ about 4,500 people or 68 percent of the county's private sector labor force.

As the volunteers completed their assignments, Mary Lee Gecowets and Jack Sommers met each week to review the surveys, focusing on the concerns, problems, or requests mentioned by firms. Each of these items was addressed either by Sommers and Gecowets or by the steering committee. Although a consultant for the program was not officially named, Paul Clapsaddle from Columbia Gas played this role as the program evolved. Clapsaddle, who was a member of the steering committee, assisted Gecowets and Sommers and the rest of the steering committee with follow-up on the survey information. In current programs, consultants are nominated before each program begins and are responsible for following up on nonlocal issues mentioned in the survey.

ACCOMPLISHMENTS FROM THE FOLLOW-UP WORK

While the coordinator and consultant frequently handle the short-run follow-up work, this was impossible in Champaign County. Although Roland Patzer had acted as the coordinator since the start of the program, he became very ill during the summer. Although his recovery was quick, in fact in time to preside over the final meeting during which the results of the program were announced to the community, Gecowets and Sommers became co-coordinators and they concentrated on the follow-up work.

As a result of the visitation program the steering committee was able to address several concerns of local industry. Some of these concerns were addressed immediately while others will require years to address fully.

Immediate Follow-Up

During one of the visits, a plastics manufacturer (injection molder) complained to the volunteer visitors about a street light in front of its plant. The light was situated such that it illuminated not the entrance to the plant but the railroad tracks running along the plant and bisecting the street. At times, truck drivers, unfamiliar with the plant location, would drive toward the light and railroad tracks thinking that area was the entrance to the plant. There was a real possibility of injury to the drivers and damage to the trucks and shipments because the entrance was so poorly lighted.

Notified of this dangerous situation, Gecowets and Sommers (acting as co-coordinators) discussed the problem with the management of the local utility company who agreed to move the street light so that it illuminated the entrance to the plant. Another plastics manufacturer shares this entrance, so two industries, employing a total of about 250 employees, benefited from this follow-up work.

During another visit, a small machining operation employing fifteen people complained to the volunteer visitors that its sewer rate seemed unusually high. This information was taken to the city, which investigated the claim. The firm's grievance was correct; the rate was too high and it was subsequently reduced.

During many of the visits, industries requested information about various subjects, such as state regulations, marketing, and labor-management relations. The steering committee responded to each request by sending information to the industries. In all, nine fact sheets were sent to industries about new state regulations, two about financing programs, two about local government services, and one about export marketing opportunities.

During the course of the program, news that stricter waste-management regulations were being proposed by the Environmental Protection Agency (EPA) reached several industries located near Mad River, a cold-water habitat in the county. These new regulations, if adopted, would significantly increase waste-management costs for these industries.

Roland Patzer and Mary Lee Gecowets attended a formal hearing at the county courthouse about the proposed regulations. Acting as representatives for the local industries, they argued that the environmental impact from these industries did not require stricter regulations for Mad River, that, in fact, the proposed regulations were overly protective of the cold-water habitat. As a result of their efforts, the proposed stricter regulations were relaxed somewhat. Although the approved regulations did increase the industries' waste-management costs, the increase was lower than it would have been if the original proposed regulations had been adopted.

Long-Term Follow-Up

The results of the survey indicated that industries wanted to see the development of a bypass road to direct traffic from the downtown area. Currently, State Route 68 (north-south) passes through Urbana, the county seat. Members of the steering committee met with the head of the Ohio Department of Transportation concerning this issue. From that discussion, the members realized that the construction of a bypass is at least ten years away. Although the state owns the right-of-way for the bypass, naturalists are strongly opposed to the construction because it would apparently destroy a bog, which is a poorly drained area rich with flora characteristic of that environment. Although the construction of the bypass is still years away, the issue pairs developers against naturalists and will likely generate heated debate, so the steering committee will continue to pursue the issue.

During the visitation program, four industries complained about a bridge in the industrial park area in Urbana. The bridge is too narrow for two trucks to pass simultaneously. In addition, it was built with a high arch making it impossible for an approaching driver to see over the apex. As a result, two trucks can approach the bridge from either direction and not see each other until they are on the bridge, which increases the possibility of a collision. Furthermore, the bridge has a restricted weight limit that prevents some trucks from crossing it. Each of these factors impedes the transportation of shipments to industries located in the park.

Members of the steering committee have approached the railroad, city, and county concerning the bridge. As of yet, however, none of these entities will assume responsibility. Despite this obstacle, the steering committee is in the process of bringing together all three players to resolve this situation for the industries.

RECOMMENDATIONS

Based on the data analysis of the survey information, the steering committee wrote nine recommendations for future economic development in Champaign County. These recommendations appeared, along with the survey results and some supplemental data from secondary sources, in the final report for the program. The recommendations were presented to the community during a Rotary Club meeting in October 1986.

Since that meeting, several of the recommendations have been implemented. The status of each recommendation is given below.

Recommendation: Creating an Economic Development Council and Hiring a Director

Based on the survey findings, the steering committee recognized the need to continue a systematic and structured approach to local economic development. The committee recommended the formation of a "Champaign County Economic Development Council." The council will include leaders from various towns and villages in the county and from various organizations so that different political, industrial, and economic interests will have representation. One of the council's main responsibilities will be to implement several of the other recommendations described below.

IMPLEMENTATION. The steering committee forms the council that was to have been in place by October 1987. The steering committee expected it to be operating by the beginning of 1988. Meanwhile, the county has hired a part-time economic development director (Gecowets) for one year. Her main responsibility is to continue following up on issues and problems revealed during the visitation program. The decision to continue this position will be made after a review of the first year's progress.

Recommendation: Providing Up-to-Date Information

Based on the findings that many firms wanted information about state and federal development programs and were considering expansion, the steering committee recommended the development of a long-range economic development plan, the continuation of the visitation program at regular intervals, and the continuation of follow-up work on the long-term issues (i.e., the bypass and bridge) mentioned by firms during this program.

IMPLEMENTATION. The Economic Development Council will implement these recommendations as soon as it is operating, probably in early 1988. In the meantime, the economic development director is continuing to address issues cited during the program.

Recommendation: Reducing Economic Leakages

From the data analysis of the survey information, the steering committee realized the need to reduce economic leakages from its industry, that is, to try to stimulate more local linkages, specifically input or backward linkages. To accomplish this, the committee recommended the development of a plan to identify the supplies and services required by local industry, with the intention of providing those inputs and services locally. Also, it recommended the continuation of Industrial Awareness Days, which are sponsored by the Chamber of Commerce.

IMPLEMENTATION. To implement these recommendations, the steering committee organized the first countywide "Business Expo" for the spring of 1988. Unlike Industrial Awareness Shows, which have been held regularly in the cities of the county, this event will be countywide, will include not only manufacturers but also businesses services and agricultural operations, and will be aimed at informing not only the community about its local businesses but also local businesses about each other.

Recommendation: Presenting Education Programs

Many of the industries visited requested information about state and federal economic development programs. To provide up-to-date information about these programs to industry, the steering committee recommended the sponsoring of an Economic Development Teleconference Series, the establishment of a directory of experts to advise business and industry about specific programs, and the sponsorship by local service clubs of speakers representing these programs.

IMPLEMENTATION. The Economic Development Teleconference Series, produced jointly by the OSU, OCES, and the Ohio Department of Development (all sponsors of the Ohio program), has been updated as of late 1987. The series consists of a dozen ten- to fifteen-minute videotapes featuring a representative from a state or federal development program. The series is designed for local industry to view the tapes to learn about these programs. After viewing, the representative on the tape is called, and via teleconference, a question-and-answer period is held.

The steering committee is currently discussing an educational program about industrial issues, such as labor-management relations, marketing strategies, land-use planning, export marketing, joint ventures, first-line supervision, and retraining options, with Clark Technical College (located in Clark County, just south of Champaign County). The steering committee plans to review similar programs and seminars offered by other colleges and agencies, but the Economic Development Council will make the final decision about which group will present this information to local industry.

Recommendation: Informing Industry of New State Regulations

Industry frequently requested information about new state regulations during the program. The steering committee recommended that the Urbana Area Chamber of Commerce should inform local industry of new state regulations through its newsletter.

IMPLEMENTATION. The chamber has included this information in its newsletter. Since this information reaches only those industries with membership to the chamber, the steering committee will begin providing this information to the local newspaper so that all industry will be informed.

OUTCOMES

In addition to the accomplishments made during the follow-up work, several other outcomes grew from the program. In retrospect, the program, which was the county's first attempt at identifying its industries' needs and concerns, provided an excellent vehicle for expressing the community's probusiness attitude. According to Gecowets, the industries visited found this program sincere, worthwhile, and mutually beneficial. Moreover, the program was a cooperative effort. It involved the support, resources, and commitment from the state, the city (Urbana), the county, private organizations, and local industry.

The program also generated more enthusiasm and local leadership within the community for economic development. Some of the volunteer visitors became more active in community events than they had before. The Rotary Club is considering sponsoring a regular Business Appreciation Dinner as a result of the program. According to Roland Patzer:

"We have accomplished several things, perhaps most importantly we have gotten community consensus for long-range planning. By participation in this program everyone agrees that we need to plan our own destiny in the future. Secondly, we hired, which is an innovative aspect for this community, a person to handle long-range planning. That person is to develop and help form an Economic Council for this county which indeed will help us in our planning. We could never have done this if it hadn't been for this particular effort. It came far quicker than many of us realized. The outpouring of financial support and the outpouring of consensus to accomplish this was a result of the R&E program and for that we have a very special thanks to give to the Extension Service for providing this opportunity."

The program also generated unexpected publicity for Champaign County. Champaign County's R&E visitation program was the focus a videotape produced by Iowa State University for the Extension Service of the U.S. Department of Agriculture. The tape was one of four presented during a national conference in May 1987. The four tapes were shown as examples of the Extension Service's efforts in economic development. The tape is an excellent tool for introducing prospective firms to Champaign County and for informing other communities of how one community approached economic development.

Lastly, the program enables leaders in Champaign County to gather information unique to its locale. Only by visiting local industry could local leaders know the actual obstacles firms must face to expand or grow, the actual criticisms industry has for the local economy, and the opinion of industry with respect to the county as a business location. Secondary data, although useful for comparison purposes and for analyzing regions, fail to provide adequate information for local development. The primary data, gathered during the R&E visitation program, however, did provide the necessary information for Champaign County to begin directing its own economic development.

Sommers, the County Extension agent, summarized the program as follows: "One of the major benefits that I have seen here locally is a lot of excitement among business and community leaders and a lot of cooperation of being creative by pulling off such a large major project with so many people being involved. We have a kind of a new attitude, a 'can-do' attitude . . . we can have a better business community, we can improve employment, and we can keep our local business growing and active within our community."

NOTES

1. While thirty-three communities did implement an R&E visitation program using the Ohio State University materials, only two prepared written reports. None of these incorporate strategic planning in their process.

11

Making Connections through R&E: An Educator's Case Study

ROBERT T. MCLAUGHLIN

This chapter reports on research conducted on an Ohio retention and expansion (R&E) program during its actual implementation.[1] The main research effort was a case study conducted in "Heartland", Ohio. The researcher conducted participant and nonparticipant observation of and interviews with the local R&E program sponsored by the Heartland County Chamber of Commerce.[2] The program process was studied from its inception to preparation of the final report. Two primary research questions were posed. First, how do the *participants themselves* define program "effectiveness"? Second, what factors do they and the researcher identify as enhancing or impeding effectiveness as it is variously defined?

The study found that:

1. the program led participants to make three kinds of connections—social, political, and epistemological;
2. participants came to identify with one another as significant others;
3. the local business owners and managers visited by program volunteers, according to program participants, were most agreeably surprised by the appreciation expressed to them;

4. the program led to more efficient flows of information by which local business-related sector leaders learn of and respond to local firms' concerns; and
5. most importantly, the net result was a considerable change in the manner in which local development policy decisions are made.

The conclusion is that the business R&E strategy should become a familiar tool in the local development actor's repertoire. This strategy:

1. involves minimal expense, because it relies heavily on volunteerism;
2. increases rapport and informal networking among program participants, who are leaders of local firms, chambers of commerce, development organizations, educational institutions, government agencies, and elected offices;
3. helps to address conflicts and problems generated by the conventional economic development strategy of attracting new firms; and
4. appears to improve significantly the capacity for local leaders, *as a group,* to respond efficiently and concertedly to barriers to local firm R&E.

THE STUDY

Rationale for Conducting the Study

Most statewide training programs and local R&E activities are less than five years old. There was understandably a paucity of research describing the effectiveness of these state and local efforts.

James Miller's studies of the relative growth of existing versus new firms points out the potential role of R&E (see Chapter 2). The benefit-cost research done by Morse, Wilson, and Gordon also provides evidence of the value of this strategy.

Many economists and R&E participants use quantitative indicators to gauge the effectiveness of R&E programs. Such indicators include the number of jobs retained, the number of jobs added, the number of firms prevented from closing, etc. However, it often is difficult to specify to what extent such impacts may be attributed directly or indirectly to R&E program efforts. Local R&E program personnel may identify a firm as possibly having to close or reduce its employment substantially; they may then meet with that firm's chief executive officer to identify strategies for preventing layoffs or firm closure. If indeed that firm survives without reducing the number of jobs it generates locally, ought R&E program personnel claim that their efforts "saved" the firm? Could not demographic, technological, market, and other forces have been the chief

factors in enabling the firm to retain the local jobs? In order to develop
methods for assessing local R&E program effectiveness, more needs to
be understood about how participants enact local R&E program
objectives. The organizational, social, and economic factors that influence
attainment of the R&E objectives should be identified. R&E programs
involve many participants, and the results of their efforts are influenced
by innumerable factors external to the R&E program itself. Research was
needed to determine which internal and external factors are most salient
in determining effectiveness.

In addition, more clarity was seen as needed in defining what
"effectiveness" means as it pertains to R&E programs. Does it mean the
number of programs started or completed? Is it the increased capacity of
local leaders to assist firms? Is it the net growth of local firms and
employment?

The local volunteers who receive R&E training could be expected, it
was felt, to have different expectations and motivations concerning their
own participation in the R&E process. To what extent are their personal
objectives consistent with the formal objectives described in the literature
on R&E programs? A program that is "successful" or "effective" for some
constituencies might not be considered so by others. Alternatively, a given
local program conceivably might be considered effective by all constituencies, yet the different constituencies may have varied reasons and
criteria for finding the program to be effective. Indeed, it was considered,
it could well be that a program universally regarded as successful may be
able to achieve this acclaim precisely because program participants have
been able to define and enact the local program so that it is seen as
consistent with the differing demands and values of diverse constituencies.

Prior to this study the researcher speculated that research could
discover that the participants in a local program may need to accomplish
more than the Ohio R&E program's five formal objectives in order to
attain the basic goals of retaining and expanding local employment and
income. To reiterate, these objectives are: (1) demonstrating a probusiness attitude; (2) solving firms' problems with local governments; (3)
helping firms use state and federal programs; (4) collecting business data
for strategic economic planning; and (5) acquiring early warning of
business closures. This research was undertaken, in part, to describe how
state and local participants perceive the reasons for their own participation. The researcher hoped that this would enable the development of a
more comprehensive concept of program effectiveness.

It was deemed that research was needed, in conclusion, to consider
both how "effectiveness" is defined as well as what factors enhance or
impede it. The overriding aim of this study was to generate a theory of
the factors inhibiting and enhancing local program effectiveness, as
effectiveness is variously defined by program participants. The aim,
therefore, was neither to test such theory empirically through this

research, nor to conduct an evaluation of the extent to which local R&E programs fulfilled the five formal program objectives. Instead, the purpose was to develop a theory by which future researchers could measure and predict program effectiveness, where such evaluation criteria would be grounded in the range of expectations and evaluation criteria employed by the participants.

The Research Questions

The central questions to be addressed by the research therefore were:

1. What are the criteria used by program participants for assessing R&E program effectiveness? and
2. What factors appear most salient in enhancing or impeding such effectiveness as it is variously defined?

THE RESEARCH METHODOLOGY

Data collection began in early August 1986 and ended in April 1987. During this time a variety of data collection procedures were employed: participant observation, nonparticipant observation, interviewing, and the review of written documentation.

Most of the data gathered for this chapter were drawn from a local program in an Ohio county that we shall call "Heartland." The case study there involved the various participants and stakeholders of Heartland's R&E program. Heartland's program began shortly after the study started so that it was possible to witness the program's evolution from initiation to completion and interpretation of its business visitation survey. Through in-depth scrutiny of this local program the researcher hoped to identify the ways in which program effectiveness was defined and to determine the kinds of factors that enhanced or impeded effectiveness as it was variously defined.

The research was conducted in three phases:

1. Long-distance telephone interviews with coordinators of local R&E programs in Georgia, Idaho, Iowa, New Jersey, and Wisconsin,
2. Personal interviews with local R&E program coordinators in Ohio, and
3. Extensive personal interviews with and observation of participants in one local Ohio R&E program.

The first phase was intended to orient the researcher to the diversity of program tactics, outcomes, and environmental factors. The second phase was to enable the researcher to select an appropriate site for the third phase of intensive case study. The third phase was designed to generate rich information regarding participants' perceptions and explanations of program effectiveness.

The third phase began in October 1986. During the period from this time to May 1987 the researcher:

1. interviewed thirty participants in Heartland's program;
2. observed six meetings of program participants; and
3. observed three business visitations by program participants.

Over two thousand pages of field notes and interview transcripts were generated. The researcher elected to perform all of the transcription himself, to maximize accuracy and his familiarity with the data.

The researcher spent a total of fourteen full days on-site in Heartland County and three days on-site in Dale County. In addition, the researcher made frequent visits of shorter duration to both sites. The schedule of questions guiding the interviews and observation changed as the researcher's understanding increased and new questions emerged. Interviews and observation were complemented by collection of program documents and historical information. Readers interested in examining the research methodology in greater detail are urged strongly to review Chapter III of the author's dissertation.

FINDINGS

Background: A Description of Heartland County

Heartland County is located in central Ohio. All of the field observations and personal interviews were conducted in person in Heartland County. The county's population, according to the most recent census figures, is under 38,000 persons. Fewer than 4 percent of the population are of minority status; this small proportion has remained constant during the past fifteen years. Studies show that the county population both grew as well as aged slightly faster than did adjacent counties.

Located within the rolling hills of central Ohio, Heartland County is a rural area. Blessed with good soil for farming, the county also possesses a wide variety of historical and recreational attractions. Beneath the surface tranquility, however, various forces stir. First, there has been a modest but perceptible outmigration of youths. Second, the mix of the local economy has changed. After two decades of decline in employment generated by recreation activities, the county is beginning to experience a significant resurgence. With the recent successful attraction of "Asiatic, Ltd." into the county, there has been a marked increase in the proportion of employment generated by manufacturing concerns.

However, the county's per capita income remained nearly 20 percent below the average for Ohio's counties. The median family income of Heartland families was more than $3,000 less than the state median. There are significantly higher proportions of farm and blue collar workers in the county and significantly fewer white collar jobs. Unemployment has tended to be consistently higher than the Ohio average during the 1980s. As recently as September 1986, Ohio Bureau of Employment Services placed the county's official unemployment rate at almost 10 percent, up from 8 percent in 1980.

Despite these employment and income figures, however, Heartland County provides no evidence of poverty, either in its principal town and county seat, "Cobbletown," or in the small municipalities and farming areas. The majority of the county's residents own their own homes, whose unpretentious architecture reflects their owners' straightforward conservatism.

The great majority of the county's voters are Republican, as were those who participated in its R&E program. Such conservatism, however, should not be mistaken as a fear of innovation. The county, in fact, has been the home of surprisingly many inventors. Interestingly, some of the first stations of the "underground railroad" were to be found in this county.

Reflecting an apparently long-standing inclination toward innovation, then, the county's development history indicates a kind of cautious aggressiveness. Leaders in local development efforts pointed to their recent success in attracting Asiatic, Ltd., a major employer.

Of particular relevance to an understanding of business R&E, the county had been moderately successful in attracting new firms while not having suffered a significant outmigration of manufacturing firms. In other words, local leaders were not motivated to participate in the R&E program because they had experienced any dramatic loss or outmigration of firms. Instead, as they said time and again, they wanted to initiate the program principally to tell local firms of their appreciation for the jobs and income that the companies had been generating for a long time.

Ironically, the somewhat aggressive approach taken by development leaders, they said, had heightened the need to show attention to existing local firms. The influx of Asiatic, Ltd. and of a number of smaller, spin-off industries had caused some illwill among existing firms for two reasons. First, the owners and managers of existing firms were seen as often resenting how "new firms get all the attention." Second, they were known to have lost valued personnel to the new, often better-paying firms. This is the context in which Heartland County's R&E program was initiated.

Heartland's Deviation: Task Force Review of the Surveys

Due to the convergence of several factors, the Heartland task force decided that it, as a group, would review each of the completed survey forms. Ordinarily, the local coordinator reviews every completed form, referring only special or unusually delicate problems for task force consideration. The decision was made because (1) the initiators each preferred to make decisions by consensus rather than by hierarchical fiat; and (2) the initiators subscribed to a *diffuse leadership* orientation. That is, they wanted task force members to share program power and information fairly equally, rather than having power concentrated among a select few. Reinforcing this orientation toward leadership, the program coordinator—a retired executive who had been selected primarily due to his altruism, business experience, and free time—had had little prior experience in managing service programs and volunteer activities. It was therefore felt that the combined knowledge and expertise of the task force would complement usefully the coordinator's capacity to respond to the surveys.

The data suggest that the task force members experienced a sense of personal "ownership" of and central participation in the program process, and that this sense was fairly equally shared among most of the task force members. This finding merits further explanation:

1. Heartland's four program initiators appeared to view themselves as having fairly equal decision-making status and authority.
2. The initiators also viewed those whom they personally recruited as having comparable status and authority.
3. Three of the four initiators appeared to prefer a consensual, nonhierarchical approach to decision-making. The fourth initiator demonstrated a preference for hierarchical decision-making but felt, for a variety of reasons, he did not have ethical or practical justification to himself adopt or encourage others to employ a hierarchical approach.
4. Among the persons who had been recruited by an initiator were those who preferred hierarchical decision-making and those who tended to decide by consensus. Yet, they all appeared to feel that insofar as they themselves had not initiated the program, they were constrained from making or encouraging hierarchical decisions because they did not "own" the program.
5. Those who had been recruited to participate by other non-initiators appeared to experience a similar constraint.

The deviation from the prescribed procedures for survey review proved to increase the relative extent to which, compared to other local R&E programs, Heartland's task force members developed a sense of trust in each other and developed more open channels of communication with one another regarding local firms' problems and their own organizations' performance relative to these problems. To summarize findings considered at length below, in *every one* of the local programs studied, task force members were reported to have experienced increased trust in one another and more efficient communication regarding development-related matters. However, these outcomes were especially noticeable in Heartland. This may well be due to the decision for the entire task force to review each completed survey.

The one significant danger in task force review of the surveys, however, is that the confidential information recorded about local firms might be revealed to the detriment of the firms. The researcher was unable to uncover any instance of such damaging revelation. This appeared to be because the task force members were authentically committed to helping the local firms and therefore had created a norm of honoring the confidentiality ethic. However, the potential for breaching confidentiality clearly existed.[3]

However, the benefits of full task force review of each survey are so significant that Morse, in response to this study's findings, redesigned his statewide training program in order to encourage others to emulate Heartland's innovation. To minimize the risk to confidentiality, Morse now prescribes that the coordinator remove identifying information from each survey form before distributing copies of the completed forms for task force review. Early indications are that this tactic is protecting confidentiality while facilitating the highly positive group dynamics of task force review.

Participant Rationales for Participating

Visitation volunteers and task force members alike, both in Heartland and elsewhere, each consistently expressed most or all of the following reasons for having agreed to participate.

1. It is "safe" to participate in the R&E program. One task force member, owner of a small firm, said "I just can't see *any* risk in getting involved in this. How can you *possibly* lose?"
2. At worst, the local program would generate positive feelings and public relations among government, business, and other participating organizations.
3. Any positive findings identified by the survey of local firms could be used to attract new firms and to enhance local civic pride among the general populace.
4. The program would meet a widely recognized need to "bring people together" to address matters of specifically local concern.
5. One has a "civic duty" to participate in this volunteer effort to "benefit the whole community."
6. Solving the problems articulated by local firms should help these firms to remain and grow in the community, thereby creating more jobs and a better local tax base.
7. Helping existing local firms, through one's program participation, would result in indirect economic benefits to oneself.

8. Participating in the program probably would be "educational" as it would give the participant the opportunity to learn about who is conducting business in the community and what goods and services the firms provide.

9. Program participation should prove "enjoyable," participants predicted, because they could socialize with other influential community members, participate in making important decisions affecting community well-being, learn about innovative ideas, and tell others about what one's own organization does and one's role in it. Nearly every participant described the enjoyment they anticipated experiencing in the program.

10. Participating in the program would allow one the opportunity to promote one's own organization—to community leaders during task force meetings, and to business executives during business visitations.

11. Most owners and managers of existing local firms were seen as probably feeling neglected and unappreciated. Participants wanted them to feel more appreciated, both for the pragmatic reasons of retaining and expanding existing firms as well as because they felt the business representatives did not "deserve to feel this way," as one respondent put it.

These varied reasons for responding positively when recruited may be classified into four kinds of motivations for participation.

1. *Organizational.* Each of the initiators also seemed to be motivated by a desire to further the aims of the organizations by which they were respectively employed. They each perceived their employers as potentially benefiting through their own involvement in the R&E program.

2. *Affective.* The initiators indicated they expected their participation to be "fun," "enjoyable," and "a real learning experience."

3. *Philosophical.* The initiators all believed in the values implicit and explicit in the R&E program as it was initially presented for their preprogram consideration.

4. *Altruistic.* Each of the initiators appeared to be motivated, in part, by a desire to be of service to others.

Interestingly, *participants were very reluctant during the early stages of the program to describe any other than organizational and affective reasons for choosing to participate.* Participants were *very* reluctant to articulate altruistic motivations—and when they did so, it was generally with *considerable* awkwardness and only in the latter stages of the program. Consistent with the thesis of Bellah et al. in *Habits of the Heart* (1985), participants lacked a comfortable language with which to express and explain their noticeably altruistic intentions.

The participants displayed considerable commitment to and investment (in time, attention, and energy) in their R&E program—beyond that
which would appear motivated by expected or potential benefits to
themselves and their organizations. The researcher concludes that *the
R&E program was able to tap a reservoir of otherwise latent altruism within
the community.*

Perceived Attributes of Local Sectors

During the early stages of the program, participants often articulated
explicit and implicit characterizations of those working in the community
sectors of business, education, government, and politics. Below is a table
summarizing these characterizations.

TABLE 11.1. Perceived Attributes of Local Sectors

Business	Education	Government	Politics
Negative			
Selfish	Impractical	Unresponsive	Conniving
	Not instill good	Incompetent	Partisan
	values	Lazy	Aloof, distant
	Too idealistic		
Positive			
Practical	Service-oriented	Service-oriented	Able to get
Productive	Idealistic		things done
Creative			
Risk-taking			

The characterizations that others attributed to one's sector, interestingly, coincided fairly closely with how one characterized one's own
sector. These characterizations were noted because the researcher
speculated, *a priori*, that a program such as R&E that prescribes the
expression of a "probusiness attitude" might exacerbate tensions regarding
the degree of sectoral credibility. For example, might a strongly probusiness effort not diminish the already limited credibility with which
political officials tend to be viewed by local development-related actors?

These typifications are noted here because the findings were
diametrically opposed to the researcher's expectations. Not only did the
program experience *not* lead participants to characterize nonbusiness
sectors more negatively but, more remarkably, the experience *improved*
the image of these local sectors. By the conclusion of the Heartland
program, the task force members and other program participants were
much less inclined to characterize one another's sectors negatively. Why?

A number of reasons may be inferred from the data, each of which has significance in its own right. These reasons have to do with the way in which the local R&E process leads to changing norms of accountability.

Norms of Accountability

The local R&E process tends to result in altered norms concerning the means by which local developed-related organizational leaders hold one another accountable in a community. The dynamics by which this occurs are discussed below.

The R&E task force provides a safe, private arena in which leaders from the local sectors can convene to discuss development-related matters openly yet confidentially.

By reviewing each completed visitation survey in the task force meeting forum, these leaders had an unusual opportunity to view one another in the process of interpreting and responding to specific local problems. Outside of the R&E task force arena, local leaders have very few opportunities to observe one another *during* the decision process.

To the extent that every local R&E program entails the review of at least some visitation surveys by the task force, all of these programs provide this otherwise rare opportunity. In Heartland, the task force review of all completed survey forms heightened this program impact.

Task force members frequently found that a given survey form revealed information critical of a particular local development-related organization, *whose leader participated in the task force.* The next survey similarly might reveal information critical of another task force member's organization. Task force members in Heartland's and other programs repeatedly mentioned the trust which developed among task force members as they reviewed such complaints and problems. The consistent tendency among task force members appears to be to institute certain *norms of accountability*, which, to say the least, are otherwise rare among the wide network of leaders involved in R&E programs.

The norms of accountability were such that task force members typically developed a norm of seeking to avoid *embarrassing* one another. The task force came to constitute an intimate arena such that members *identified with* one another. Heartland's task force members were seen repeatedly to avoid criticizing one another for problems, real or alleged, which firms were reported to have attributed to a task force member's organization.

Task force discussion of problems recorded in the surveys provided members with an opportunity to discuss what their respective organizations could and could not do. Local leaders rarely have the opportunity to explain in any detail the constraints upon and capabilities of their agencies. Through such communication others were able to develop *more realistic expectations regarding organizational capabilities.*

On the other hand, because of a generally authentic commitment to resolving local firms' problems where possible, task force members did apply overt and subtle pressure upon one another to resolve and prevent problems in the future. That is, although they did not blame one another for past mistakes, they implied in countless ways that avoidable future mistakes would prove embarrassing. The researcher cannot overemphasize the intensity of the desire of task force members to avoid such embarrassment.

The task force provides an arena in which, to summarize, *identification-with* accountability dynamics become operant to a greater degree than is likely otherwise to be found among the leaders of most American communities. This form of accountability is one in which: (1) rich information about an organization's leader is generated and considered; (2) one empathizes with—i.e., imagines oneself as filling the role of—that leader; (3) one becomes reluctant to condemn that leader for this or that inadequacy; and, perhaps most significantly, (4) one recognizes that in an interdependent community, one shares responsibility for the extent to which another is able to perform satisfactorily.

This form of accountability needs to be contrasted with that of *identification-of.* The aphorism, "familiarity breeds contempt," comes to mind here. The ideal means of assessing and enforcing compliance with social expectations—as found both in the policy sciences literature as well as in the politics of most American communities—is through identification-of. It is identification-of cognition, it is posited here, rather than identification-with, that breeds contempt.

Identification-with accountability relies upon: (1) empathy; (2) the collection and interpretation of rich qualitative information regarding organizational performance; (3) the intimacy of a nonpublic arena for discussing organizational performance, and (4) embarrassment to enforce compliance. Identification-of accountability utilizes other means. This more orthodox approach to accountability typically involves: (1) the objectification of the persons whose effectiveness is being assessed; (2) the creation of quantitative criteria against which to measure performance; (3) the required dissemination of performance numbers in a public arena; and (4) the imposition of legalized sanctions and regulations to enforce compliance.

Over the course of the R&E process, task force members and, to a lesser extent, visitation volunteers (who are generally less intensively involved in the program), come to identify with one another increasingly closely. The task force thus becomes somewhat akin to the "breakfast club" form of leadership network found in most communities. In a breakfast club, members know one another well and tend to appreciate the full range of forces which limit the capacity of one another's organizations to resolve local firms' concerns. However, where a breakfast club tends to consist of a small circle of the community's elite, the R&E program design prescribes the recruitment of a more diversified group of local development-related leaders. This prescription appears to reduce the exclusionary and elitist tendencies of the local leadership network.

Two other design features impose pressure upon R&E task force members to authentically improve the quality of their organizations' support to local firms. First, where many breakfast clubs lack powerful *external* constituencies to which they are accountable, the R&E task force is explicitly accountable to the firms their volunteers have visited. These firms—each a major local manufacturer or other large employer—have considerable "clout" both singly and in the aggregate. Program participants often expressed the view that these firms' owners and managers expected more than "lip service" attention to their needs. While participants were instructed to promise only that they would *try* to resolve firms' concerns, the visitation process nonetheless generated a strong expectation among business leaders that the attention and efforts would be authentic.

Second, the program prescription requires that the local task force produce, announce, and disseminate a final report. This report presents the aggregate survey results. Even a cursory reading provides diverse local constituencies with considerable information with which to inquire about the performance of the community's development-related organizations and leaders. Thus, compared to the breakfast club network, the R&E task force constitutes a network which is at once more open, more inclusive, and subject to external scrutiny.

To be sure, however, the local R&E task force is a somewhat exclusionary body, as its members are drawn typically from the ranks of local professionals and decision makers. This should not diminish the fact that the R&E process nonetheless moves a community toward a less representative and more participatory democracy—at least with respect to local development decisions concerning the community's firms.

Fragmentation and the R&E Process

After the expression of a fear of embarrassment, concern about the *fragmentation* of local development decision processes was the single most commonly voiced sentiment among program participants. Local development-related organizations were viewed as not having informed or been informed by one another's plans or concerns. Across all local development sectors, leaders said they felt that the uncoordinated approach to local development led to unnecessary negative externalities, inefficiency, duplication of effort, and even sometimes conflict.

The R&E process was seen to lead not only to *coordination,* but also to *cooperative coordination.* The former term is meant to connote coordination that is achieved largely through rationalized forms of communication and interaction. Cooperative coordination, on the other hand, may involve more or less rationality but also involves relatively intimate, identification-with forms of interaction and communication. Participants initially hoped or expected that the program would remedy the fragmentation of development decision-making through simple coordination. By the end of the program, in Heartland and in every other program studied, many participants came to enthuse that cooperative coordination had been achieved.

Making Connections

The Heartland R&E program resulted in participants, particularly task force members, making three sorts of "connections"—social, epistemological, and political. These are summarized below.

New *social connections* were made in that task force members came generally to identify much more closely with one another than they had prior to the program. Equally, through the face-to-face interaction of the business visitations, many visitation volunteers commented that they had come to "better appreciate" (or, identify with) the circumstances in which the owners and managers they visited must operate.

New *epistemological connections* were generated in that participants came to view local development-related activities and aspirations as far more *interdependent* than they previously had seen them to be. In the early stages of the program process, Heartland participants spoke in general terms of the ways in which one's economic well-being depends upon that of others. By completion of the program, participants were describing, in unsolicited commentary, a wide variety of specific ways in which their well-being was interdependent with that of specific other individuals, firms, and economic sectors.

In other words, where initially participants viewed themselves as interdependent with generalized others, they later viewed this interdependence as with significant others. This latter sense of interdependence appears central to the concept of "community," it should be noted.

In addition to a shift in overall perspective regarding the quality of interdependence, another major epistemological change was in the store of descriptive information regarding specific firms and other program participants, and their respective needs, capabilities, personalities, and aspirations. The visitation process, not insignificantly, generated numerous requests that information be supplied to firms and that a wide variety of concerns and complaints be addressed.

New *political connections* were fostered in that: (1) local development leaders came to make decisions through more cooperatively coordinated and consensual rather than fragmented ways; (2) decisions now were more likely to be made based on values that were shared by their fellow development leaders; (3) the network of persons permitted to influence the substance of development decisions was widened appreciably; and (4) leaders gained a richer understanding of the constraints and capabilities that each other brought to development endeavors.

Post-Program Vehicles for Orchestrating Development

Heartland's task force, upon completion of the final report, decided to secure funds with which to finance the recruitment of a full-time development professional. They determined that this was needed to carry out plans and programs developed by the task force. They decided that the informal task force would continue meeting periodically as an *informal* working "committee."

In every R&E program studied, the local R&E task force concluded that some formal or informal organizational vehicle needed to be employed to sustain the cooperative coordination fostered by the R&E process. This in itself is significant. In other words, a consistent outcome of the local programs studied was that participants chose to sustain the cooperative coordination they had begun to experience.

In addition, the participants consistently expressed their assessment that *the R&E process* facilitates *the attraction of new firms but, unlike conventional economic development strategies, does not do so at the sometimes disastrous expense of existing local firms.* Firm recruitment sometimes, as with Heartland's attraction of Asiatic, Ltd., creates substantial problems for existing firms. By discerning and heeding the interests of existing firms *before* seeking to attract new firms, one increases the likelihood that the new firms will be ones whose needs and operations are *complementary* to the interests of the existing businesses.

ON THE IMPACTS OF EXPRESSING APPRECIATION

Local program participants in Heartland and elsewhere repeatedly expressed how surprised the firm owners and managers they visited were to be thanked for generating employment and income. A moment's reflection suggests that business leaders are rarely thanked—unless it is for providing some form of pro-bono or philanthropic contribution. The selectivity with which business leaders typically are thanked suggests a profoundly negative implicit message: business leaders should be thanked *not* for what they do every day, but only if and when they do something *other* than generate jobs and income.

As a self-perceived humanist, the researcher began this research with an expectation, possibly common to humanists, that any program so avowedly "probusiness" could not be entirely good. Would not the pro-business message central to the program concept simply serve to further legitimate the essential selfishness and competitiveness of American business? The researcher—in the parlance of qualitative research—sought to "bracket" this bias. That is, he sought to be aware of it in order to prevent it from biasing the data he sought and the way in which he interpreted it.

Fortunately, the data not only confounded but also irrefutably contradicted his expectation. The expression of appreciation by visitation volunteers was profoundly welcomed by the firm owners and managers. They were known to respond in exceptionally warm and positive terms to this appreciation. One participant offered the provocative thesis that thanking business leaders for doing what they normally do—i.e., make money—would better encourage these leaders to become more involved in community service and philanthropic endeavors.

Where the business sector is negatively characterized, it has been noted, it is in terms of "selfishness." However, might not many local business leaders who are averse to playing a greater role in community service endeavors feel discouraged from doing so *because* they feel misunderstood, ignored, and unappreciated? Implicitly accused of being utilitarian, most business leaders are thanked, in a utilitarian fashion, only in order to elicit their extraordinary support.

The R&E dialogue between business representatives and volunteers, of which many of the latter are drawn from nonprofit sectors, contains messages of appreciation which are simultaneously ends-in-themselves as well as of instrumental value. That is, the visitation volunteers expressed an awareness that the expression of their appreciation would and was intended to foster various positive outcomes, such as a reduced inclination to relocate one's firm. However, they also expressed the conviction that the message of appreciation should be expressed *for its own sake*—simply because, as one respondent said, "they *deserve* to be thanked."

Economists speak of both economic as well as "noneconomic" factors as determining decisions regarding firm creation, expansion and relocation. The expression of appreciation is a noneconomic factor whose importance should not be underestimated.

NOTES

1. The author wishes to thank the Ford Foundation, the Aspen Institute for Humanistic Studies, and the North Central Regional Center for Rural Development for grant support that made the research reported in this chapter possible. Readers wishing a fuller account of the study's findings are referred to the author's dissertation, from which excerpts have been taken for this chapter.

2. "Heartland" is a pseudonym selected to protect the confidentiality of key respondents.

3. For this reason George Morse, State Program Director, tried unsuccessfully to dissuade the group from using this procedure.

REFERENCES

Ady, Robert M. "Shifting Factors in Plant Location." In *Shaping the Local Economy.* Ed. C. A. Farr. Washington, D.C.: International City Management Association, 1984.

Bellah, Roger, R. Madsen, W. Sullivan, A. Swidler, and S. Tipton. *Habits of the Heart: Individualism and Commitment in American Life.* New York: Harper & Row, 1985.

McLaughlin, Robert. "Four Levels of Disagreement about International Development." *Futures Research Quarterly* 2(2) (1986): 33–52.

___. *Making Connections in the Heartland: An Educator's Case Study of a Local Business Retention Expansion Program.* Ph.D. Diss., Ohio State University, 1987.

___. "On the Effectiveness of Local Business R&E Programs: An Educator's Perspective." Presentation at national conference, Rural Development Strategies for the 80's: A Training Conference, sponsored by the National Association of State Agencies, and cosponsored by the Midwest Research Institute and the National Association of Development Organizations, Dec. 1–2, 1986, Lexington, Kentucky.

Miller, James P. "Expansion and Retention of Existing Businesses in the Great Lakes states: 1976–1980." Presented at Community Economic Development by R&E of Existing Businesses. Conference conducted at Ohio State University, Columbus, Ohio, Oct. 1985.

Morse, George W. "The Benefits and Costs of Retention and Expansion Visitation Programs." Presented at Community Economic *Development by Retention and Expansion of Existing Businesses.* Conference conducted at Ohio State University, Columbus, Oh., October 1985.

Morse, George W., Kathryn Wilson, and Steven I. Gordon. *Local Industry Visitation Programs: Policy Research and Recommendations.* Report prepared for the Ohio Labor Management Committee and the Urban Affairs Program. Columbus, Oh.: Ohio State University, Dept. of Agricultural Economics and Rural Sociology, March 1985.

Otto, Daniel. "States' Educational Programs for Local R&E Strategies." Presented at Community Economic Development by R&E of Existing Businesses. Conference conducted at Ohio State University, Columbus, Ohio, Oct. 1985.

Pulver, Glen. "A Theoretical Framework for the Analysis of Community Economic Development Policy Options." In *Nonmetropolitan Growth and Community Change.* Ed. F. Summers and A. Selvik. Lexington, Mass.: Lexington Books, 1985.

Schon, Daniel. *The Reflective Practitioner: How Professionals Think in Action.* New York: Basic, 1983.

Vaughan, Roger. *Early Warning Systems for Retention and Expansion of Existing Firms.* Urban Consortium Information Bulletin. Washington, D.C.: U.S. Dept. of Commerce, 1981.

12

Coping with Failure in Retention and Expansion: Plant Adjustment Approaches

MARION T. BENTLEY

Hardly a week goes by without the media reporting another plant closing that results in massive job losses and economic dislocation. While perhaps the steel and auto industries have been the most visibly affected, textiles, chemicals, electronics, rubber, timber, footwear, and mining, among others, have also suffered devastating losses. Through the 1980s, our national and regional economies are restructuring themselves. Heavy manufacturing, once the showcase of industrialization, has fallen prey to forces reshaping the marketplace as we prepare to enter the twenty-first century.

While all R&E programs hope to prevent plant closures and/or major contractions, this is not always possible. Some plants cannot be retained. This chapter examines and compares shutdown options and highlights the role to be played by third-party facilitators such as R&E programs.

What happens to workers when massive layoffs or plant closures remove them from their place of employment? How many of these workers return to the same or similar jobs as economic conditions improve? How many remain unemployed or discouraged or eventually settle for different and usually lower paying jobs? These and other questions were raised and answered by a special household survey conducted by the U.S. Department of Labor in 1984.[1] Among the

183

principal findings:

- A total of 11.5 million workers, twenty years of age and over, lost jobs because of plant closings or layoffs between January 1979 and January 1984. Those who had worked at least three years on the job—the focus of the study—numbered 5.1 million.
- The profile of the 5.1 million workers who had been displaced from their jobs fit the conventional description. They were primarily men of prime working age, had lost typical factory jobs, were heavily concentrated in the Midwest and other areas with heavy industry, and if reemployed, were likely to have shifted to other jobs, occupations, and industries.
- About 3.5 million of the displaced workers had collected unemployment benefits after losing their jobs. Nearly one-half of these had exhausted their benefits.
- Many no longer had health insurance coverage, including some who subsequently found work.
- About 3.1 million displaced workers were reemployed by January 1984, but 50 percent were working in different industries, about 1.3 million were still looking for work, and the remaining 700,000 had left the labor force.
- Of the 3.1 million reemployed workers, about half were earning as much or more in the jobs they held when surveyed than in the ones they had lost. Many others, however, had taken pay cuts that often exceeded 30 percent.
- Blacks accounted for about 600,000 of the 5.1 million displaced workers and Hispanics about 300,000. The proportion reemployed as of January 1984 was relatively small for both groups—42 percent for Blacks and 52 percent for Hispanics.

In communities throughout the nation, local elected officials, development practitioners, social and community agencies, and concerned citizens faced with plant closings that involve hundreds, sometimes thousands, of jobs struggle to develop and implement an appropriate response to economic loss and worker hardship. What can community leaders do to save jobs or create new ones when a company announces its intention to close a factory, mine, or plant? The impact is almost always serious, often traumatic, as the loss of primary jobs leads domino-like to the loss of secondary and support jobs and ultimately to diminished community revenues and capacity for coping with dislocation.

Faced with prospects by high unemployment and mounting social costs, community leaders and affected workers often struggle independently and in isolation to cope with the effects of massive dislocation—jobs, income maintenance, housing, insurance benefits, retraining, counseling—physical, financial, and emotional loss. It needn't be so. All affected parties, including workers, employers, and communities working together can achieve much greater success than any one party acting independently.

The response to the closure of a factory or plant might vary from doing absolutely nothing to providing a comprehensive menu of services to workers and the community. Given the wide range of specific responses, it is helpful to group assistance strategies into general categories:

1. Laissez faire
2. Labor-management directed
3. Community directed
4. State or federal approaches

The Laissez Faire Strategy to Plant Closings

While easily the most frequent response to a facility closing or mass layoff, the first category of assistance strategies is not helpful in dealing with the consequences of dislocation. Laissez faire is no strategy at all. The scenario follows a typical pattern.

The parent conglomerate, usually from a remote home office, announces one day that a well-established local factory is no longer competitive. Typically, the handwriting has been on the wall for years. The machinery is outmoded; the company's more modern factories are using newer equipment, and nothing foreshadows a shutdown like failure to reinvest. The workers usually have been told to hold down wages or the plant will have to move; the town has been warned that property taxes must be abated or they will lose the plant altogether. Often these demands have been met.[2]

But the dreaded day arrives anyway. Workers are told on Friday not to come to work on Monday. Minimal provisions are made for extending severance pay or health insurance benefits and none at all for counseling, training, and other assistance services. The burden of the closure falls most heavily on the displaced workers and their families. All too often, the community lacks direction or commitment; it can't decide whether the closure is the responsibility of the city or the county, or the employment service or social services, and so does nothing of a systematic comprehensive or strategic nature.

The other three categories of assistance strategies offer genuine insights and guidelines for action and seem to show an increasing awareness of responsibility and commitment on the part of employers, unions, communities, federal and state governments, and interested third parties.

The Labor/Management Approach to Plant Closings

The basic joint labor-management approach has evolved over the past three decades to help employers and unions deal with plant closings. The recent Ford Motor Company–UAW jointly negotiated approach represents an outstanding application of the labor-management directed model for closing a facility or dealing with major permanent work force reductions.[3] The basic elements of the Ford–UAW model are based on the 1982 collective bargaining agreement:

1. Six months advance notice of closure
2. Distribution of contractually stipulated benefits to displaced workers (severance benefits, SUB benefits, continuation of health insurance, preferential placement at other Ford plants)
3. Full joint union-management involvement in the planning and implementation of programs developed
4. Technical assistance and financial support are made available from the UAW–Ford National Training and Development Center
5. Full cooperation is given to and appropriate use made of public agencies and services
6. Local autonomy through the creation of a local joint labor-management committee, an Employee Development and Training Program Committee through which all decisions and actions are initiated

The primary functions of the EDTP committee involve the following:

1. Organize an employment and retraining center at the plant or nearby premises
2. Staff the center with qualified training coordinators
3. Coordinate closely with plant management regarding the phase-out of plant operations
4. Arrange for participation of other public and private agencies such as job service, adult and community education, vocational education, and social services
5. Write proposals for funding
6. Advise and counsel displaced workers
7. Arrange for the delivery of appropriate services such as orientation and benefits, assessment, testing and counseling, adult basic education, in-plant vocational exploration courses and seminars, targeted vocational training, job search training and job development, interplant transfer and job placement

In summary, the joint labor-management approach developed by Ford and UAW through EDTP committees gives joint responsibility for providing leadership and direction to the entire plant closing process as it relates to the needs of the displaced workers. The emphasis is on providing a full range of services to ensure positive career redirection, not just immediate reemployment. The results have been impressive. Fully 70 percent of the 2,500 workers displaced from the Ford San Jose assembly plant in Milpitas, California, participated in some phase of activity at the on-site training center and 30 percent received some form of training or retraining.

Dana Corporation, General Motors, Goodyear, Armour, Brown and Williamson, and International Silver Corporation are among a growing list of employers and unions that have benefited from a joint labor-management approach to close a facility. Lessons learned from these experiences suggest that successful readjustment programs share many characteristics.[4]

1. Direct involvement of affected firms and unions
2. An organized local committee or team
3. Good leadership from management, union, and community officials
4. Early notification and intervention
5. Nonbureaucratic organization approach
6. Shared resources
7. Frequent, ongoing communication
8. Employment and retraining center
9. Alternative approaches and services—cafeteria style

In those cases where the employer does not want or intend to take the full responsibility for planning and implementing as assistance program for the displaced work force, then the community represented by business and commercial interests, local elected officials, religious leaders, representatives of management of the local affected plant, local and state agency officials, and other civic and community leaders can often provide an effective vehicle for dealing with the immediate and long-range effects of the closure.

The Community-Based Approach to Plant Closings

The community-based approach provides advantages to the distressed employer and workers not usually found in the more typical, piecemeal non-joint approaches and by companies or unions or state agencies to deal with the displacement effects of plant closure. These advantages include:

1. one organization empowered to coordinate federal, state and local programs and other resources available to both workers and communities affected by a shutdown;
2. one central organization providing cohesion for what otherwise would be disparate and diffused efforts and a focus for the coordinated effort to secure funds, training, and other forms of assistance for workers, the affected plant, suppliers to the plant and users of discontinued goods and services, and the community;

3. one visible public or quasi-public organization providing tangible, valuable support to workers and the community as evidence of concern and a determination to help find answers and results; and

4. one organization charged with the identification of emerging problems and issues and potential resources available to help resolve personal, family, and community problems.

In short, a community approach to a shutdown has the potential for mobilizing and rallying public and private resources in a common cause, providing leadership and direction to a coordinated solution, and assuming rightful responsibility for the public good. Successful examples of community involvement in plant closings include Fresno and Hayward, California; Des Moines, Iowa; Hartford, Connecticut; and Southeastern Wayne County, Michigan.[5]

From the vantage point of the community several critical issues are raised. Community leaders must organize services to provide affected workers with immediate outplacement assistance—counseling, training, job development and placement. Additionally, the community must address the long-term challenges of: (1) attracting new economic activity capable of filling the gap left by the economic decline, (2) diversifying the local economic base, and (3) maintaining a healthy element for the employers who still remain. An effective strategy to deal with these issues must involve the affected employer and the larger business community.

From an organizational standpoint the issues that a community must address when confronted with the prospect of massive dislocation fall into three main categories:

1. Obtaining visibility, support, and commitment from the community and its business, labor, and civic interests

2. Deciding on a strategy or approach to use as the basis for organizing and developing the administration and management of the committee to deal with the closure and the resulting organizational problems; e.g., membership, agenda times, scope of functions, resources available for implementing recommendations, and similar management and leadership functions

3. Maintaining a sense of urgency and need with the community and the community team organized to deal with the shutdown. Once the plant actually closes it is tempting to consider the problem of the shutdown solved: the union disbands, the company leaves, town, and the unemployed retreat from sight and mind.

State and Federal Approaches to Plant Closings

The labor-management and community approaches to coping with dislocation have increased their success and effectiveness when coupled with enlightened local, state, and federal government assistance and support. Two of the best models of a public/private partnership are represented by the California Economic Adjustment Team and the Canadian Manpower Consultative Service.

The California Economic Adjustment Team (CEAT) is staffed by the directors of the state's leading agencies and institutions that provide re-employment services to dislocated workers: Employment Development Department, Department of Economic and Business Development, Department of Industrial Relations, Office of Planning and Research, Public Instruction and Community Colleges. CEAT enables the departments represented on the team to pool their resources and coordinate community, company, and labor resources to develop comprehensive procedures for workers and localities affected by plant closures.[6]

CEAT operates throughout the state of California responding to any plant closing considered major in terms of either the number of workers displaced or the economic impact on the community. Through 1984, some twenty dislocated worker programs have served more than thirty firms and 35,000 workers. Members of CEAT learn of impending plant closures through voluntary notification from the firm or through maintaining mechanisms within their agencies.

Once notified of a shutdown, CEAT determines if the problem is large enough to require the assistance of the entire team or if it can be handled by field staff. The full team usually works together on closures affecting at least 1,000 workers. It will collaborate on smaller shutdowns if the number of people displaced represents a significant portion of the labor force in the community where the plant is located. Once team members decide the full team is needed they form an oversight committee with representatives from their agencies, the affected firm, and the community. This committee designs a readjustment plan specific to the local situation and selects one of two formats through which to deliver services: the employee-based model or the community-based model. Central to every CEAT project is the displaced worker reemployment center, which offers workers a full range of personal and financial counseling, skills assessment, job search techniques, job development and retraining opportunities. These centers are typically located on-site or in the union hall where workers feel comfortable and have easy access to the services. Employee benefits, economic development strategies, and business relocation efforts are also included with the package of services provided by CEAT.

The Canadian Manpower Consultative Service (CMCS) is a unit housed within the Federal Employment and Immigration Commission of Canada. It is charged with assisting companies experiencing labor adjustment problems.[7] CMCS serves a neutral party to bring labor and management together at the company level to develop joint solutions to problems such as layoffs, plant closings and slowdowns, automation, and training for new technologies. Regional CMCS case officers contact distressed companies—Canadian law requires early notification—or occasionally a company takes the initiative and approaches CMCS regarding manpower or labor unions. Participation is voluntary. Labor and management representatives are contacted, and if they agree to jointly address the presenting issues, a committee is formed and a joint agreement developed. A Manpower Adjustment Committee is formed and a committee work plan outlined. If the problem facing the committee is a layoff, closing, or slowdown, the work plan includes: (1) delivery of information to all affected workers, inviting them to participate in placement activities; (2) assessment of need for counseling, training, referral, or relocation; (3) creation of an inventory of employee skills and work preferences; and (4) development of a job network to identify possible placements for affected workers.

The CMCS concept stresses flexibility and minimizes bureaucracy. In fact, both CEAT and CMCS share characteristics predictive of successful interventions:

1. Public/private partnership
2. Early response
3. An outside, third party catalyst
4. Locally led response
5. Growing and declining sectors linked
6. Coordination of resources

SUMMARY AND CONCLUSIONS

Whichever model is employed to address assistance and readjustment needs of the displaced, the role of the neutral, third-party facilitator or catalyst is a critical one. Certainly, general duties and responsibilities of this key figure include fostering communication among all parties, identifying community interests and needs, pinpointing employee problems and needs, locating community resources, dealing with policy problems and playing an ombudsman's role. More specifically, prospective jobs must be inventoried, relocation assistance provided, welfare assistance and income maintenance coordinated, outplacement strategies organized, training and retraining options planned, and lost economic activity replaced.

Robert McKersie and Werner Sengenberger provide additional focus to the general responsibilities of third-party facilitators.[8] Targets of efforts include both jobs and workers while forms of restructuring or readjustment are both internal and external to the firm. Improving enterprise vitality by direct cost cutting, give-backs, productivity bargaining and improvement programs, developing alternative products, and changing the ownership of the firm are examples of internal job creation or preservation targets. Internal efforts to assist workers is accomplished by implementing new human resource techniques, including reducing the numbers of workers by attrition and hiring freezes, early retirement, voluntary leave; by balancing operations with manpower buffers to handle fluctuations in work load, and inventory buffers by warehousing goods during slack demand and offering incentives to customers to stockpile during slow periods; by reducing hours, job sharing, layoff rotation, and other work sharing approaches.

Efforts to help workers external to the firm are accomplished by preparing them for labor market reentry through testing, counseling, training, retraining, placement, and other appropriate outplacement or readjustment activities.

Finally, economic development leading to new jobs created external to the affected firm is accomplished by attracting new businesses, strengthening and expanding existing businesses, targeting vocational training with existing and potential firms, and aggressively developing jobs based on common industry and skill requirements.

In order to compete in international markets, American industry must have the freedom to invest and disinvest to capitalize on strategic and comparative advantages. However, the shift in resources, "capital flight," must be buffered by equally strategic and humane approaches to assist workers who are displaced and communities that are overburdened with the consequences of disinvestment.

NOTES

1. Paul O. Flaim and Ellen Sengal, "Displaced Workers of 1979-83: How Well Have They Fared?" *Monthly Labor Review,* June 1985, 3–16.

2. Barry Bluestone and Bennett Harrison, "Why Corporations Close Profitable Plants." *Working Papers for a New Society,* Vol. 17 no. 3, May–June, 1980, 18.

3. Gary B. Hansen and Marion T. Bentley, *Closing a Plant the Ford Way: The San Jose Assembly Plant,* Logan, Utah: Utah Center for Productivity and Quality of Working Life, Utah State University, 1984.

4. Gary B. Hansen, "Ford and the UAW Have a Better Idea: A Joint Labor Management Approach to Plant Closings and Worker Retraining," *Annals of the American Academy,* Sept. 1984.

5. Gary B. Hansen and Marion T. Bentley. *Problems and Solutions in a Plant Shutdown: A Handbook for Community Involvement,* Part III. Logan, Utah: Utah Center for Productivity and Quality of Working Life, Utah State University, Nov. 1981.

6. National Alliance of Business, Bulletin, March, 1983. Information on CEAT and CMCS comes largely from this source.

7. National Alliance of Business, Bulletin, Mar. 1983.

8. Robert B. McKersie and Werner Sengenberger, *Job Losses in Major Industries: Manpower Strategy and Responses* (Paris: OECD, 1983), 62–93.

REFERENCES

Bluestone, Barry, and Bennett Harrison. "Why Corporations Close Profitable Plants." *Working Papers for a New Society,* Vol. 17, no. 3 (May–June, 1980): 18.

Flaim, Paul O., and Ellen Sengal. "Displaced Workers of 1979–83: How Well Have They Fared?", *Monthly Labor Review,* June 1985, 3–16.

Hansen, Gary B. "Ford and the UAW Have a Better Idea: A Joint Labor Management Approach to Plant Closings and Worker Retraining." *Annals of the American Academy,* Sept. 1984.

Hansen, Gary B., and Marion T. Bentley. *Closing a Plant the Ford Way: The San Jose Assembly Plant.* Logan, Utah: Utah Center for Productivity and Quality of Working Life, Utah State University, 1984.

————. *Problems and Solutions in a Plant Shutdown: A Handbook for Community Involvement.* Logan, Utah: Utah Center for Productivity and Quality of Working Life, Utah State University, November, 1981. Part III.

McKersie, Robert B., and Werner Sengenberger. *Job Losses in Major Industries: Manpower Strategy and Responses.* Paris: OECD, 1983, 62–93.

National Alliance of Business, Bulletin, Mar. 1983.

Index